Ernest Francisco Fenollosa

East and West

The Discovery of America and Other Poems

Ernest Francisco Fenollosa

East and West
The Discovery of America and Other Poems

ISBN/EAN: 9783744661614

Printed in Europe, USA, Canada, Australia, Japan

Cover: Foto ©Thomas Meinert / pixelio.de

More available books at **www.hansebooks.com**

EAST AND WEST
THE DISCOVERY OF AMERICA AND OTHER POEMS BY ERNEST FRANCISCO FENOLLOSA

NEW YORK 46 EAST 14TH STREET
THOMAS Y CROWELL AND COMPANY
BOSTON 100 PURCHASE STREET
M D CCC XCIII

COPYRIGHT, 1893,
BY T. Y. CROWELL & CO.

Norwood Press:
J. S. Cushing & Co. — Berwick & Smith.
Boston, Mass., U.S.A.

Each solemn sweet truth
　Is indited to thee,
Dear playmate of youth,
　Who a-perch on my knee
Heard me proudly rehearse —
　With a kiss for a dash —
From my first callow verse; —
　Heard the far billows plash
To our nest in the East,
　Where we learned from the doves
How to chant, like a priest,
　At the shrine of our loves.

Each dainty light thought
　I have written for thee,
O little one brought
　Like a pearl from the sea;
Who lay in a basket
　Rose-blown to the South,
While rhymes in a casket
　Were caught from thy mouth.
Should after-years query,
　My laurel of fame
Shall rest with thee, dearie,
　Who bearest my name.

PREFACE.

In "East and West" I have endeavored to condense my experiences of two hemispheres, and my study of their history. The synthesis of two continental civilizations, matured apart through fifteen hundred years, will mark this close of our century as an unique dramatic epoch in human affairs. At the end of a great cycle the two halves of the world come together for the final creation of man.

This union was foreshadowed two thousand years ago in the swift career of Alexander the Great, when, at a blow, he brought the arts of Greece face to face with the mystical thought of India. In the Hellenic kingdoms the ancient types of East and West were mingled to the point of a vital exchange of faculty. But, with the decrepitude of the Roman Empire, Europe and Asia, bearing in their bosoms this pledge of plighted troth, withdrew into that long seclusion the barriers of which should not be broken until the might of invention could go hand in hand with sympathy.

Eastern culture, slowly elaborated, has held to ideals whose refinement seems markedly feminine. For it social institutions are the positive harmonies of a life of brotherhood. Western culture, on the contrary, has held to ideals whose strength seems markedly masculine. For it law is the compromise of Liberty with her own excesses, while conquest, science, and industry are but parallel channels for the overflow of hungry personality.

But this one-sidedness has been partly compensated by the religious life of each. The violence of the West has been softened by the feminine faith of love, renunciation, obedience, salvation from without. It is the very impersonality of her great ecclesiastical institute which offers to man a refuge from self. On the other hand, the peaceful impotence of the East has been spurred by her martial faith of spiritual knighthood, self-reliance, salvation from within. The intense individuality of her esoteric discipline upholds the fertile tranquillity of her surface. This stupendous double antithesis seems to me the most significant fact in all history. The future union of the types may thus be symbolized as a twofold marriage.

Meanwhile the first attempts to assimilate alien ideals have led to the irony of a quadruple confusion, analogous to the disruption of Alexander's conquest. But our genuine interest in music predicts our native power to compass a profounder integration. Within the coming century the blended strength of Scientific Analysis and Spiritual Wisdom should wed for eternity the blended grace of Æsthetic Synthesis and Spiritual Love.

In "The Discovery of America" I was governed by two aims: one, to expand the resources of poetic art by the inspiring analogies of music; the other, to exhibit the steadfast idealism of Columbus as the medium through which overshadowing Spirit achieved its sublime purpose of uniting the East and the West. To-day his triumphant caravels have met the ambassadors of Xipangu on the shores of Lake Michigan.

Steadfast as he, I cling to the faith that a frank recognition of the great, illuminating, spiritual verities, realized by the vivid flash of the imagination, is, and has been always, in art the only profound realism.

ERNEST FRANCISCO FENOLLOSA.

BOSTON, October 15, 1893.

CONTENTS.

EAST AND WEST.

		PAGE
PART I.	The First Meeting of East and West	3
PART II.	The Separated East	14
PART III.	The Separated West	29
PART IV.	The Present Meeting of East and West	39
PART V.	The Future Union of East and West	48

MINOR POEMS.

PASTORAL	59
DECEMBER	60
THE HOUR	61
REQUIEM	62
THE DRYAD	63
ON OPENING AN ALBUM	64
THE SOUL QUESTIONS	66
THE GOLDEN AGE	68
THE SNOWDROP	71
LOVE'S YOUTH	72
SONNET: MY PERFECT TRUTH	74
SONNET: MY SACRIFICE	75
SONNET: FUJI AT SUNRISE	76

CONTENTS.

MINOR POEMS—*continued.*

	PAGE
SONNET: HER LOVE	77
REPROACH	78
THE WOOD-DOVE	81
SEPTEMBER	83
NEW YEAR'S EVE, 1875	85
GOD'S FORESTS	90
LOVE AND MUSIC	95
AT HER TOMB	98
TELEPATHY	100
REVERIE	103
IN THE AURA	105
SONG OF THE WIND	107
THE CAPTIVE	112
KARMA	114
MAYA	117
MAYTIME	122
WITH DEATH	125
SPRING BREATH	128
IN NORWAY	130

THE DISCOVERY OF AMERICA. A SYMPHONIC POEM.

FIRST MOVEMENT: The Sea and the Sky	137
SECOND MOVEMENT: Dreams	151
THIRD MOVEMENT: Wedding Music	169
FOURTH MOVEMENT: Triumph	185

EAST AND WEST

*A POEM DELIVERED BEFORE THE PHI BETA KAPPA
SOCIETY AT HARVARD UNIVERSITY*

JUNE 30, 1892

EAST AND WEST.

PART I.

The First Meeting of East and West.

YET once again discordant trumpets blare
To mar the music of the hemispheres.

So heard the ancient world a cry of doom,
Of agony which blossomed into prayer,
And saw the laden treasuries of years
Spilled on the flaming altar of her tomb.

Fragrant the memory of Arcadian flutes,
And shepherds' dance in groves whose Orphic lutes
Flood space with tune; of Jove's Olympian plains
Where strive earth's naked gods; and gilded fanes
Carving warm outline from Corinthian skies;
Or cool Castalian depths where mystery lies;
Or the broad terraces of Parthenon
Crowned with the sunflash from the virgin's shield,
Whose proud chivalric bloom of Attic field
In dance of throbbing marbles surges on

As Phidias dreamed, that prince of centuries
On his immortal throne, Acropolis.

And aromatic music yet distils
In languid drops through soil of Indian lore,
Echoes which cling like moss to temple floor: —
The tinkling bell of Aryan upland kine
Calling to prayer the herdsman, nature's priest;
And that great martial pageant of the East
Where Krishna preached of peace; and palaces
Of Sakyan kings upon a hundred hills
Fringing the skirts of Ganges — sacred foam
Wherein the Brahmin bathes — till Ocean's brine
Swallows her floods of prayer; the rock-hewn dome
Hung with blue veils of incense, and gray stones
Where weeping saints lay the last Buddha's bones.

Perchance these two sweet songs took soul and shape
One evening when the low sun held his breath,
And Nature, pausing as at thought of death,
Played with her folded canopy of crêpe.
Then the delirious waves which flood the halls
Of Time subsided; and, with vision clear,
Floating as in a crystal atmosphere,
Two wingéd spirits spake at intervals: —

"Mark how the shuttles of the falling stars
Weave golden fabrics on the warp of earth!
How their soft patterns swing

Like birds upon the wing;—
Of our fair faces mirrors, as a brook
Wherein two lovers look!
How plastic universes wax and wane,
Tangles of Brahma's skein,
Where rainbow thoughts come flushing to the birth,
And the pale gold of Venus melts in the blaze of Mars!"

"Spirit of Beauty, see
Thy crown transferred to me,
The heritage of Western orbs which sink
Beyond Olympus' brink;—
Through the long night which shuts upon the world
A downy seedling curled
In thy rich soil thick sown with shattered gods;
But as a pale white blossom
Nursed in the fragrant moisture of this bosom,
From which again shall start
The tender shoots of Art,
Fresh fronds of perfect curve like ends of tunes,
And groves of graceful palms to fleck our sods
With the long shadows of the Eastern moons."

"Soul of the East, I kneel
Thine inmost mood to feel.
Heart, as of woman, wet
With the first dews of nature's morning dream,
Here on this cold hard brow in mercy set
Thy sacred touch, and break

This chain of sparkling jewels which I deem
A bond upon my soul; and in thy lake
Of childlike self-unfolding consciousness
Baptize my soul with floods of sweet distress.
Show me reflected shades of sacrifice,
And opal tints of pity, and cloud forms
Of unimagined aspiration piled
Against the enamelled blue of earthly aim,
And powers without a name
Which the calm pilot of the soul enjoys
When in salt wash of seething currents wild
He steers new worlds through elemental storms."

"So may our spirits for a moment float
As in a new-built boat;
Clasping each other
With the warm love of sister and of brother,
Breathing fresh life together
From every blast of Jove-distracted weather.
For now the future glows
With the rich promise of Aurora's bows.
Now we can see all sin
And pain but as the flesh we struggle in;
Let perish pleasure's sloth,
And cherish pangs of growth,
And folding hands in prayer
Welcome the futile tortures of despair:—
For the great plan of universal Law
We gaze upon with awe.

Yet is the moment done.
Black is the buried sun.
One kiss before we part,
And in the hurried mingling of our breath
Transmit the seed that shall not suffer death;
In tear-wet patience of a lonely heart
Each in his separate soil
To plant and water with long ages' toil;
Until again perhaps
Thousands of years shall lapse,
And in some second focus of God's will,
When the long night of cataclysm ceases
And worn-out worlds have torn themselves in pieces,
In some sweet dawn which dissipates that ill
We shall bring forth the pure and ripened flower
Conceived in this sweet hour.

"Yet now harsh horns begin
To rasp in din.
And all the world grows black
With gathering shadows of the coming wrack.
Away! Farewell!
And now unleash the murderous hounds of hell!"

* * * * * * * *

Reclining on his roof in Macedon,
The youthful Alexander
Heard a loud cry, and from the Eastern ocean
Saw cloud-shapes leap like warriors in commotion,

And lightning shafts hurled swift as bolts of battle,
And scouts of flying scud which hurried on
The rising tumult of the thunder's rattle.
And in the bosom of the young commander
A flame leaped up, as if a star had broken
And in a molten mass its contents poured
Through the dilating chambers of his heart;
While, Fate's grim message eager to impart,
Quick hissing in his ears Ambition roared: —

"Darling of destiny! prince of the ages!
Jove-dowered paragon! nursling of sages!
Sword of the universe! moulder of races!
Welder of hemispheres! forger of spaces!
Rise, O arise, for they fight in the skies,
And the chargers of demons have blood in their eyes,
And the captains of light, and the cohorts of shades
Are pricking the kings of the world with their blades
To yield thee the wealth of their crowns as a prize!"

Thus was the signal of the furies spoken.

* * * * * * * *

At Issus, after fateful Granicus,
In rival lines paused Greek and Persian hosts.
But high in upper strata of the air,
Tossing in wild disorder, mutinous,
Like the torn fringes of a Typhon's hair,
Lay two o'ershadowing armaments of ghosts,
Mighty contingents from all unseen spheres.

The morning sun lit up their ranks of spears
With myriad flashes, like magnetic glances
Shot from arched forests of auroral lances.
But their tumultuous rings were held in curb
By two archangels, arrogant, superb,
Fierce spirits of the elemental fire
Who sped on eager wing at Jove's desire
Down from the parching dust of Martian fields
To plan fresh woes for this distracted ball;
Calm, cruel, dread with gorgon-headed shields
Forged in the sun, and fresh Hephaestian mail.
Waved each a falchion like a comet's tail
Threatening extinction to a million stars.
And now against the drum-head of the moon
Shivered a lightning bolt; and all hell shook,
While the supreme recorder in his book
A new page marred with blood; and like a wall
Smitten with earthquake fell the impatient bars,
Whence, snorting trumpet blasts, a mad platoon
Of rampant elephants rushed forth, and raged
Down that black plain of cloud like winds uncaged;—
As Alpine peaks had avalanches hurled
Down the besplintered pathway of their rock;—
With liquid leaps, as some great torrent runs
Bursting the futile barrier of its dam,
And oscillating like a drunken world.

But lined in solid ranks to meet the shock
Knelt calm ten thousand archers, who at once

Bent their great bows as bamboo forests bend
When off the Yellow Sea beats the simoom.
Earth heard their loosened cords like crack of doom,
Or the last crash of some mad orchestra.
And a low cloud of hissing serpents sped
Stinging like fire-fed eels from Surinam;
Till those great mammoths fell and writhed in pain,
Tearing each other's flesh, as tigers rend
The bones of sheep. And now the gilded car
Of each archangel moved; the ominous tread
Of myriad chargers sounded on their flanks;
And gathering lines of mounted furies whirled
Down either side, and tore through broken ranks
As spring-fed torrents tear through rock-choked passes,
Sweeping away, like cyclones, struggling masses;
Till in the centre of that blood-streaked plain
They met as mountains meet, when Titans cast
Pelion on Ossa, and their fragments spurt
Through startled space a jet of asteroids.

And now the red demonic masses seething
In the wild vortex of those awful voids
Felt the strained strata of the atmospheres
Cracking beneath them; and, as polar bears
Slipping on toppling icebergs when the spring
Loosens the Greenland crust in Baffin's Bay,
They reeled, and through that crumbling crater passed
As towns melt up in earthquakes, like the spray
Of salt seas hissing through earth's molten heart.

Not like the falling Satan dazed, inert,
Impotent, cursing like a baffled king;
But as a blood-red dragon active, breathing
Mephitic tongues of flame, with teeth like swords
To reap glad harvests of barbarian hordes; —
So on the pygmy heads of Persian hosts
Thundered this dread Niagara of ghosts.

But now the Greeks like a long fire-tipped dart
Burst frontward in. And Alexander shrieked
To frenzy wrought by hell's unclaimed alliance.
And the shrill whistle of his hot defiance
Pierced, with the meteor-flashing of his blade,
Straight to Darius' heart; who turned dismayed
Into the maddened flight of plunging horses
Trampling to crimson froth their slippery courses.
As some proud orb, meeting magnetic bars
Flashed from indomitable master stars,
Pauses a moment, hesitant and piqued,
Then with a shudder hurries retrograde
Down the long reaches of the zodiac; —
So did the Persian monarch on his track;
So swirled behind the spray of rout and wrack,
Like Tigris, flooding Babylonian plains
With wreckage of undreamed catastrophe.

And now the world lay at his feet. But he,
Like some discarded engine of the gods,
Smitten by rash excess of his own Mars,

Fell on the pathway of the continents.
Not all the wingéd fates for which he fought,
Not all the gorgeous gates of ancient reigns
Submerged beneath his Macedonian sea
Could grant him shelter. Yet those peaceful waves,
Filling earth's golden cup from Chersonese
To the wide crystal of Himálya's rim,
Wearing strange channels for Ægean seas
Through Indus' mouth,— whence the returning tide
Sweeps the vast spoil of oriental thought,—
Lay on the pregnant bosom of those sods
Through the long evening mists of centuries,
The sunset chamber of the world's veiled bride;
Where dull Seleucid crimson afterglows,
Or the last purple arch of Parthian bows
Blended rich blooms from continental graves:
Lay in still depths of brooding elements
Like ferns in dark organic soil of tombs,
Whose slow gestating mystery of wombs
Silent, unheralded, in twilight dim
Moulded twin orbs for hovering cherubim.

So had the spirits of the hemispheres
Fore-planned the fruitful years,
Ere nature's cyclic chills
Should wrap their tender souls in separate ills.

So the pure germ of art
Washed from its native soil,

Warm with the last caress of Grecian toil,
Nestled against the oriental heart;
Mid the first kindling faith of Scythian plains
Found tender incarnation
In shoots of fresh creation
Creeping like frost-blown flowers o'er Buddhist fanes.

So, too, Imperial Rome,
Smitten with pangs of unsuspected birth,
By her new Eastern blade of conscience keen
Stabbed in the secret chamber of her heart,
Rent her gay robes of art,
Levelled the stately marbles of her home:
Then, with breast bared,
And gray head bent to earth
In the first ecstasy of suffering,
Rushed to the desert like a guilty thing,
And cast her weight of sin, so gladly shared,
Upon the Mercy of the Nazarene.

So shall we leave them there,
Two worlds as if in prayer,
In consecration kneeling,
For one blest moment feeling
That strife
Is not true life,
That perfect rest
Is best.

PART II.

The Separated East.

O sweet dead artist and seer, O tender prophetic priest,
Draw me aside the curtain that veils the heart of your East.

    O wing of the Empress of mountains,
    Brood white o'er a world of surprises;
    And soar to thy Sun as she rises
    From the mazarine arch of her fountains.
    For thine islands she dropped in the reeds
    As a girdle of emerald beads,
    And her rainbow promise of genius spanned
    As a bridge for the gods to their chosen land.
    And her last pure poet shall sing
    Like a farewell note
    From a nightingale's throat
    Of her peace, through thy roseate window of Spring.

    I saw him last in the solemn grove
    Where the orange temples of Kásŭga shine,
    Feeding the timorous deer that rove
    Through her tall, dark, purple pillars of pine,
    And marking the pattern of leaves

Which the golden mesh of the willow weaves
On the olive bed of her moss-grown eaves.
And I cried to my painter-sage,
"O spirit lone of a bygone age,
Smiling mid ruin and change,
With faith in the beautiful soul of things,
I would gaze on the jewels thy vision brings
From the calm interior depths of its range.
For I've flown from my West
Like a desolate bird from a broken nest
To learn thy secret of joy and rest.
Quaff from thy fancy's chalice,
And build me anew the fairy palace
With arches gilded and ceiling pearled
Where dwells the soul of thine Asian world."

Then I thought that his smile grew finer,
As if touched with an insight diviner;
Dear Hogai, my master,
Perched on a wild wistaria stem.
And I marked the light on his mantle's hem
Of a halo pure as a purple aster.
And the cold green blades of a bamboo spear
Pierced to his hand through the atmosphere,
Like the note of a silver bell to the ear.
And his voice came soft as the hymn
Which the snow-clad virgins in cloister dim
Were chanting, with rhythmical sway of limb.

"The past is the seed in the heart of a rose
Whose petalled present shall fade as it blows.
The past is the seed in the soul of man,
The infinite Now of the spirit's span.
For flesh is a flower
That blooms for an hour;
And the soul is the seed
Which determines the breed,
The past in the present
For monarch or peasant.
Eye to eye
'T is ourselves we spy;
For doom or grace
One manifold face;
Life's triumphs and errors
In self-resurrections,
Like endless reflections
From parallel mirrors.

"Now I speed on a charger of wind
To the snow-capped castles of Ind.
Mid statues of Buddha the meek,
Link between Mongol and Greek,
Kanishka haughty and lone
Here lolled on his sculptured throne,
The great Vasubandhu to mark,
Lion-faced patriarch.
Now moss like a pall
Shrouds the ruined wall;

Afar in the desert the tigers call.
One pilgrim alone
From its sandy bed
Is lifting a beautiful Buddha's head.
'O take me, loved of the dragon throne,
Back to thy pious imperial prince;
For ages and ages since
'T was I who carved that form
From the limestone warm.
I 'll show thee where germinate in the soil
A thousand truncated gods for thy spoil.
Gather these Bodhisats,
And battle-scarred features of grim Arhats,
And arrogant alabaster kings
With eyes of jacinth
Dethroned from their plinth,
And the masterful heads of Scythian knights
Scowling in mortal fights
With misshapen elemental things.
And hurry thy laden ship
On a heaven-blessed homeward trip; —
So shall the Northern and Eastern plains
Clap their hands at thy gains.
For the light of unborn states
From these things radiates;
Blood for solution
Of crystal worlds Confucian;
Stars for the final Asian man
Rising in far Japan.

I'll paint on the wall
Of thy Tartar capital
Blue gods unmoved in everlasting flame,
Vast planetary coils without a name,
Invigorating thrills
From unseen wills.
And spurred by these I shall cast
Black bronze in an infinite mould,
As high as a pine
And as fine
As the patient jeweller carves his gold;
Impersonal types which shall last
As the noblest ideals of the Past.'

* * * * * * * *

"O crystalline flash at the bar of billows!
O amethyst gate of the Eastern seas!
O balmy bosom of soft spring willows!
O pearly vision of white plum trees!

"O blest Hangchow, I fly to thee now
As a fluttering dove to her leafy home;
As the seabirds sweep o'er the spray of the deep
To the reedy fringe of Sientang's foam.

"Now a mirror of pines thy soft lake shines
By the dewy breath of the morning kissed.
And the spouting rills like the blood of the hills
Are drunk by the passionate lips of the mist.

"In a tangle of leaves with silken sleeves
 Thy poets sing on the terraced beach,
 Where the blue-flagged taverns with mossy eaves
 Are starred by the pink of the blossoming peach.

"Thy ramparts rise with roofs to the skies
 Like a jewelled cluster of golden peaks.
 'Neath the crystal ridge of the arching bridge
 Is the dreamy shade which the boatman seeks.

"While sunbeams play on the rock-hewn way
 To the dizzy heights of his temple's spire,
 Like a spirit roves in mountain groves
 The priestly painter with soul a-fire.

"Nor frost of age shall the saintly sage
 Restrain from the balm of his walk at noon;
 Nor the hem of the night retard the flight
 Of the maiden who bares her breast to the moon.

"In dainty dells where the silver bells
 Of far-off temples caress the breeze,
 Shall nature's child with her locks blown wild
 Her herbs let fall as she falls on her knees.

"For visions come on the noontide hum
 Of soul in the infinite warmth of things,
 The mirror of moods where spirit broods
 With the glory of love on her half-grown wings.

"There knotted pines with their storm-torn lines
  Are stamped with the stress of a passion human;
  And the willow swims on its current of limbs
  Like the yielding heart of a queenly woman.

"And mountains crossed by the track of the frost,
  And rocks that harden with weight of woes,
  And rivers that hide like a sweet, shy bride,
  And thorns which sting in the kiss of a rose,

"And habits that twine in a clinging vine,
  And innocent herons in lotus beds,
  And water that showers the vernal flowers,
  Are the patterns of soul with its rainbow threads.

"And a song of pity is rife in the city;
  And the marts of toil are a revel of mirth;
  And the passion of labor is help to a neighbor
  For the sake of the love God breathes on the earth.

"Let the painter paint a world for a saint!
  Let the poet sing of the realm of the heart!
  Where the spur of duty is the passion for beauty
  There Love is a law, and the Law is an art.

"O crystalline flash at the bar of billows,
  O tremulous secret the pine-trees hum!
  There once was a life like the peace of thy willows,—
  But night shuts down, and my voice is dumb.

* * * * * * * *

"Farewell to the dawn in the meadow!
Farewell to the glint on the dew!
All hail to the wing of the shadow,
And a kiss for the curse of the new!
'T is the flight of the wild goose graven
On the pale green gold of the West;
And I wake to the call of the raven.
Let me sing to the land of my rest!

"O land where the towns are like garden blooms!
O land where the maids are like peaches!
O gardens faint with their own perfumes!
O maidens like waves on the beaches!
O erratic child Japanese!
Heir of Mongolian peace,
Though we know not thy fate hereafter,
Thank God for thy genuine laughter.
Bathe in the passing mood of thy mirth
As in sunlit ether the earth;
Like the plunging bow of a ship
In the pools of thy faith still dip;
And freshen the Asian ideal
In the cooling floods of the real.

"Not for sages only
Or hermits lonely
Blows the bud of truth;
But for innocent youth,
Hearts that smile
With no shadow of guile.

Let pink-veined pleasure bloom!
Bliss
Like the kiss
Of a summer air,
Roving it knows not where,
Blessing it cares not whom!
Words
Like the glad good morning of the birds;
Loves
Like the coo of doves;
Soft whispers
As of fair nuns at vespers;
Airs
Pure as a child's first prayers!
Let us dance
To the moon
In a ring of wild flowers!
In a trance
Let us swoon
On the lap of the hours!
Let us fly
Like a lark to the sky!
Let us graze
Like a dove-eyed fawn
On the purple pastures of haze!
Let us leap on the gem-starred lawn
Of the virginal dawn!
Let us gaze
In a pool

In the heart of a dell
Shady and cool;
On the film of that well
See unexpected
Beauty reflected,
The world of art
Like a thing apart; —
Ripples of notes
From wild birds throats,
Blurred outlines
Of the shimmer of pines,
Tangled masses
Of dew-soaked grasses,
Faint perfumes
From the mirrored blooms!
This is thy mission,
O child of transition,
To illumine the gloomy pages
Of later ages.
Retain simplicity
Even to eccentricity,
Prize individuality
As man's divinest quality,
The spontaneity
Of Deity!
Teach them the music fine
In the curve of a perfect line;
Teach them to water their art
With the blood of the heart!

"O happy children of blest Japan,
  Relics of elemental man
  Before souls wilt
  In the parching consciousness of guilt!
  Dance to the tune of thy flutes,
  Or weep at thy pathos of lutes;
  Gather like laughing stars
  Round the course of thy festal cars;
  Light the smoking torch
  O'er the flower-bed in thy porch;
  Hang evergreen
  On the gate at New Year's e'en;
  Love storks and deer
  And all things significant and queer;
  Wine cups of buds like myrtles,
  And the hairy tails of turtles,
  Pigeons feasting on temple crumbs,
  The explosive eloquence of plums;
  Crowds picnicking merry
  In snowy vistas of cherry,
  Where perfumed avalanches
  Slip from the laden branches;
  Leap of the carp
  To strike the wistaria's harp,
  Garlands to deck the brow
  Of the marble cow;
  The pleasant croon
  Of far secluded priests at noon
  Gliding o'er lacquered floors,

Pacing long lines of orange corridors,
Where the dim gold Buddh of the altars
Nods to the hum of their psalters!
In the very incense smoke
Consecrate thy harmless joke;
Banter of paradoxes,
Folk-lore of badgers and foxes;
Fathers of families
Preaching droll homilies;
Children in merry hosts
Frightened by masks of ghosts,
Toasting rice-cakes on winter nights,
Battling with saw-stringed kites,
Sisters and brothers
Basking like kittens in the love of their mothers!

"O mother heart, pierced with keen
Anxieties that banish sleep
For sons who rove on the deep,
Pray to the holy snow-white Queen,
Spirit of Providence,
Choosing her throne
On the cold gray stone,
In love intense
Sweeping with inner sense
O'er miles of watery waste,
Rushing in haste
Where cold billows lift monstrous lips
To suck in blasted hulls of ships!

Pray for the golden peace
Of the Buddha of Infinite Light!
Let the importunity cease
Of the Self who knocks in the night!
Make thy choice
Of the low inarticulate voice!
Save the man at thy breast
Who screams
At the sting of the gold in his dreams,
The unholy strife of the West!"

* * * * * * * *

O wing of the Empress of mountains!
So sang thy last poet at Kásŭga's fountains.
The chant of the vestals had ceased.
The moon was awake in the East.
The love-locked pine-branches o'er us
Tinkled their bells in sympathetic chorus;
And the willow wept
Where the violet smiled as she slept.
My heart too was swelling
With the tears of a love past telling.
But I said:—
" O blossom of life in a dew-starred bed,
Thou art too sweet for this earth,
Too exquisite to linger;
Like the peace of a blest babe who dies at birth,
Like the agony of tears

When the young mother robbed of its prayed-for
    years
Kisses the listless finger.
Say, on the feminine curves of thy plain
Rises no rock for a counter-strain?
Are there no trumpets to shriek
In the sleeping ear of the meek?
No comet to threaten the sun?"
Yes, there was one; —
One priest white-robed who seemed to glide
Like a ghost from the rock at my side,
With a smile that pierced like a sword
And a soul-compelling word.
And I heard him say,
As we fell on our knees to pray: —

"The fire of combat flashes
'Neath the grass-grown slopes of the ashes.
The planets are held in their places
By the struggles of mighty races.
Choice souls have forever come
To be trained for their martyrdom
Since the days when Kukai hurled
His dart from the Chinese world.
What can the dreaming people know
Of the tempest surging below,
Of the devils storming the very
Fort of the monastery?
He who would strangle an elf

Must first of all conquer himself;
The true knight
With his own heart fight,
Antagony
Of untold agony!
On no external god relying,
Self-armed, heaven and hell alike defying,
Lonely,
With bare will only,
Biting his bitter blood-stained sod; —
This for the *world*, as for Japan,
This is to be a man!
This is to be a god!"

PART III.

The Separated West.

Soul of my inner face, face of my race,
Strong mask of self-assertion, positive,
Firm lip of competition, masculine,
Broad brow of Mercury, quick, cunning, keen,
Fierce eye of Mars with crest of sunlit fringe!
Through nights of Time I mark thy luminous course,
Furrowing rich worlds with prow piratical,
Grafting new shoots on broken racial stems,
Sowing old soils fresh fertilized with blood.
Thou art the sieve of men, whence weaker bulks
Slip through the meshes to oblivion.
Breathe through my blood once more thy feverish glow,
Long chilled by cooling crusts of compromise;
Thou, strong in reciprocity of needs,
Expansive self-willed personality!

Standing upon the vantage-ground of peaks
Kissed by the light of rising Easter dawns,
I mark long lines of shadows surge like ghosts
Waging with noiseless shout their mimic war.

As some vast wave o'ertopping lunar tides,
Engendered at the bottom of the sea
By stifled monsters wrenched, whose fissured mouths
Feed on her protoplasmic gelatines,
Sweeps on with circling rim, like living discs
Of light from stars long centuries extinct,
Slipping from pole to pole as if a hand
Caressed the tiny surface of this ball; —
So from dark mouths of prehistoric woods
Which once had reared their gloomy palisades
To hail the slow retreat of baffled ice,
Issue chill floods of melting Northern snows,
A wild Teutonic wave of glacial steel
Submerging Roman worlds; with surge of spray
Mocking the lonely sentinels of Alps,
Cresting the faithful bar of Apennines,
Storming the portals of the Pyrenees,
Tainting the sunlit laughter of the Rhine
With eddying crimson shrieks of tortured hearts; —
A flood of human fiends, by furies driven
To quaff the wine of life from lipless skulls,
And doom for slaves fair weeping captive maids
In marts of their own marble palaces.

Now shot from polar coasts see meteors flash,
Long lines of viking ships, with low black hulls
Like vultures, plunging through the Northern seas,
Hovering like gulls in track of channel storms,
Scouring for prey the long white sunlit cliffs;

Wailing their chant to Odin like wild winds
Surging through organ pipes of naked fiords,
Wooing Valhalla to Northumbrian hills
Or primrose-garnished banks of lovely Seine.
Now, drunk with richer wine of vanquished worlds,
Wielding the cross as once their bolt of Thor,
They skirt with gorgeous sweep Hispania's curves,
Through pillared gateway of the land-locked sea
Set in its rifted coasts of gilded cloud,
A blue enamelled dragon! Now they break,
Those strange Norse champions of a Hebrew god,
The threatening onsets of the Saracen,
Dispersed like storms which strew with wrecks thy coast,
Nurse of a hundred races, Sicily!

Whether in corpse-choked pass at Roncesvalles,
Second Thermopylæ of Paladins;
Or in the vortex of Valkyrian joy
Welcoming Hastings' maddest hail of spears;
Anon in flaming wrath of wild crusades
Storming the hoary walls of Constantine,
Laying a clanging wreath of naked swords
Upon the tombstone of the Prince of Peace;
Forging new thrones for kings pontifical,
Wresting dominion from the polar ice,
Filching the torrid spoil of Indian seas;
Columbus with his unaccustomed keels
Piercing the void to worlds antipodal:—
Whether it be, in song, Arthurian knights,

Or Siegfried battling with the wills of gods,
Or weird still voices of the steel-clad maid;
Now the atomic flash of feudal war,
Now the red arguments of Christian zeal;
Or where in gloomy dungeons of the soul
Shrieks the self-torture of inquisitors;
Or where in glow of young creative faith
Pure Gothic pinnacles like crystal darts
Precipitate on films of firmament,
Echoes of martial songs to melt in tears,
Passions of hearts to palpitate in flowers,
Fire-whorls to lap the altars of the moon: —
There I accept my dower of Western blood
Kneeling in sackcloth as a penitent
To consecrate such power for worthier aim.

What gave this world of turbulence its strength?
What its cement of bonds centripetal?
Was it blind crash of molecules supreme
Compelling peace of equilibrium?
Tangles of selves in planetary coils
Won from vast voids of human nebulæ?
Force bearding force like John at Runnymede?
Rights torn like blasted profiles from the rock?
Self abdicating self for self's own aim?
Ah, Law, laugh loud at heaven's harmonic code,
Then kneel to naked negativity!
Cromwell and Luther hail as champions,
Not Him of Galilee thy guarantee!

O self-fed spring of thought, O eager lip
Of scientific pride, thou too art stained
With the ancestral curse; — analysis
Splitting ideas in fine-spun silver threads
Like the cold drip from icicles, impelled
To wrest each numbered angle from the maze
Of cosmic synthesis, all faiths and loves
To solve in pools of fleshly impulses;
Sweeping the sky with rival telescopes
For paltry gold or crumbling stars of fame,
Yet in the blindness of self-centred zeal
Founding new plinths for shafts of spirit-worlds.
Whether in wars where words like bolts are hurled
From ramparts of scholastic fortresses,
Or systems crashing from their Titan suns
To fall in spray of blasted principle;
Or gnomes who dig dark secrets from the earth,
Or sylphs who mount the coursers of the clouds,
Ariels who hail the shadow of the moon
For cyclic chase of self-hid photospheres;
Bees bearing message from the bursting buds,
Adventurous birds, earth's floral pioneers,
Or boys who cast away the wanton stone
To marvel at the lithesome leap of life;
Whether the faultless search that stifles pain,
Or incarnating thought which lifts on high
Vast airy webs of steel to span the floods,
Rivets the ends of earth with breathing links,
And laughs at space in telepathic speed;

Or be it libraries of bygone deeds
Rescued from torch of time, or mysteries
Of interracial flux, or desert wastes
Of dry statistic covering fertile wells: —
These be thy choicest blooms for offering
Before the judges of Manwantaras,
Thou, thirst unslaked of curiosity!
Thou, prying, piercing pygmy, unappalled
Though hell launch forth anathemas, resolved
To conquer facts as thou destroyest worlds!
Thou dauntless Norseman steering fragile barks
Into the sunsets of Infinity!

Now on high noon of hot commercial tides
See thy ripe products borne to Eastern spheres;
Threatening the world with thy belligerent types,
Threatening thyself with thine excess of zeal.
The very lust and greed by which is spun
The knitting tissue of these cruel wounds,
The very curse which whips our naked crews
To span the world with steel-bound leap of trade,
Poison the crimson life-tide of our veins,
Convene the dread tribunal of our doom.
The smoke of chimneys taints this verdant world.
The pests of crowded indigence and vice
Are nigh to eat the manhood of thy heart.
See'st thou the fuse of thine own dynamite?
Self-law, self-science, self-greed, self-wealth, self-sworn
To blast the stanchest stronghold of thy pride!

The West provokes the East.   The iron arm
Slips off the narrow edges of this world.
Flaxen-haired vandals hunt for zest of blood
The black striped tigers of the Bengalee,
Scaling the slippery crests of Himavats,
Holding the poisoned cup to Mongol lips.
See in last glimpse how unchecked years condense
The forces of destruction. — Miles of wall
Gemmed like enamelled rainbows, gleam of lakes
Shot through fair parks, whose lines of granite bridge
Sweep like the sculptured drapery of a god;
Cresting the hill a dream of jewelled tents
Caught from the mirror of the sunset skies,
Now crystallized in marble terraces,
And gilded pillars, and the arch of roofs
Bright with chromatic coronet of tiles,
And endless treasures of green-hearted bronze,
And blood-red urns, and rare canary sheens
Flashed from a whispering sea of draperies; —
The Summer Palace of the Dragon Throne
Unmatched by all the wonders of the world; —
Now lapped in flame, whose red remorseful lip
Shrinks from the dread repast, pillars of smoke
Bearing earth's funeral wail to weeping stars
For the lost marvel of the centuries; —
Like crumbling glow of Alexandria's tomes
Or shattered fragments of the Parthenon!

Ah night that falls
In floods of twisted palls,
Blot out this culminating crime of men;
For far on high
In yon polluted sky
Meet the two spirits of the world again.

"Brother, for this
Gave I my parting kiss?
Is this the flower
Nursed in thy bosom from that fateful hour?
Two thousand years
Wasted to drown the world in tears?
Where is the gem
Of broken-souled contrition,
The victory of submission,
I lent thee from my Eastern diadem?"

Then spake the angel of the West,
With tear-wet wings folded upon his breast: —
"Sister, it is not lost,
That flame of Pentecost.
It burns
In the still spirits of my chosen urns.
What though through age-long nights of violence
The masculinity intense
Of races rude
May desecrate its mood?
I can reveal to thee another story

Of apostolic glory; —
Prayers that have curbed
The brutal passion of a world disturbed,
For wild despair the vent
Of pity's sacrament,
Love as a balm
For torn and bleeding souls,
As of a bell that tolls
Notes of eternal calm!
Canst thou not feel
The stricken millions kneel
Clasping the bloody cross whereon He dies?
Praying for torture keen,
The crown of sacrifice
Upon the cold brow of their Nazarene?
Hast thou not seen
The tenderest human loves which Raphael paints,
Transports of saints
The angelic brother limned
Kneeling in ecstasy with eyes tear-dimmed?
Tears for that stricken mother-soul's baptism,
Her coronation's chrism,
The intrinsic, fertile, pure divinity
Of Spirit-wrapped Virginity!"

"Yea, brother, thine the pain
Of wounds not dealt in vain.
Again, O plighted heart,
We meet, no more to part.

For thee I've kept
These tender buds of art,
For thee I've wept
O'er worlds that smiled like maidens as they slept.
Now my reward supreme
The manhood of thy dream!

"But there's a deeper bliss
We must not miss.
Hear'st not the signal spreading
News of a second secret wedding?
Religious rites
Of holy nuptial nights?
Dost thou not hear it,
Virginal wife of my spirit?
I am indeed the spouse
Shall lead *thee* to my house.
O tender Christian love,
O tear-blest dove,
I am thy husband's eye,
Through which thou shalt descry
Planes of angelic power
Reserved for thy last dower!"

"Hear, earth, our song,
For thou art bidden
To double nuptials hidden!
And thy confusion shall not last for long."

PART IV.

The Present Meeting of East and West.

Let us mount! let us mount! 'T is the spur of the horn!
Let us leap like a lark in the face of the morn!
Let us vault over hedges or rank river-edges,
And annihilate space in the rage of our race!
Come, prince, like a varlet bedeck thee in scarlet;
Come, ply the great trade of this mad masquerade,
Like a harlequin's prance or a dervish's dance!
For we hunt, for we grope for the phantoms of hope,
And we blow a wild kiss to the scoffing abyss; —
Not for gold; — for we 're told that 's the curse of the
        bold!
Not for love; — she 's a fool that we read of in school!
Then for fame? — Not a bit! It 's as hollow as wit!
But we hunt, and we hunt all the same. It 's a game!
It 's for madness of blood that we ride on the flood.
And we would, if we could, leap the girdle
Of the infinite sea like a hurdle!

O you West in the East like the slime of a beast,
Why must you devour that exquisite flower?
Why poison the peace of the far Japanese?
Is there no one to tell of the birthright they sell?

Must they sweat at machines like a slave to the means,
And murder the ends at the beck of false friends?
As the heart of a cloud shall the meadow of Asia be ploughed
By the curse of your fire, and the glare of your selfish desire!
    A fig for their artists and scholars!
    We crave the dry-rot of their dollars.
    We teach them to live in dark palaces.
    We lend them the sting of our malices.
    We preach them the practical Buddha of Self,
    And civilization the deification of pelf,
    The infinite snarl of sectarian watch-dogs religious,
And spiteful revenge, and the sword of a spirit litigious,
And a taste for the gaudy grotesque and the pompous prodigious.
    O spirit of Genghis Khan
Come, whirl through the circus of debt with your runaway span!
    See Tamerlane,
He lies in the corner unhorsed by the lance of champagne!
    Beware, the Centaurian daughters of Tartars
    May trip in their garters!
    New navies in armor
Are forged from the blood-weight of rice;
    And the food of the farmer
    Is sold at the throw of the dice.
And decent despair in black coat stalks abroad through the land.

The devil, he prays in good English, and swears like a
 gentleman grand.
　And here come art-students with honors!
　They graduate strictly in marble madonnas.
No more shall their panels be carved with a lily grotesque.
They swear by the natural Raphaelesque arabesque;
Cut anchors for stencils,
And round up a portrait with Christian lead-pencils,
　Improving the mighty Napoleon
　With phrenology slightly Mongolian.
　Child of some blind bewildered bard
　Learning Sunday-school tunes by the yard!
　Sons of earth's supplest dancers
　To graduate in the Lancers!
　Friends of idolatrous priests
　Converted in time for strawberry feasts!
　Confucius indeed!
　A dried-up old seed!
They know of the prigs and the canting professors who
 came of that breed!
　And Roshi who looks at the cracks
　On terrapins' backs!
Why, they blush as they think of the foxes they used to
 avoid in the stacks!
And Buddha, with baubles and bubbles of principles
 easily blowable? —
No, thank you! Philosophers rightly prefer the Unknow-
 able!

　　　*　　*　　*　　*　　*　　*　　*　　*

O you East in the West,
What is true?   What is best?
You buzz with absurd speculation, and break up the pride
of our rest.
We thought we had got to the bottom of evil, and sickness, and charity.
Don't speak of a Carpenter's Son! It reveals a too painful disparity!

O civilization on the verge of salvation,
Exposed to perfection of nature's selection,
Let us thank men of money that the world is so funny!
Let us shout for the wings that are sprouting on kings!
Let us peep through the prism of their sly optimism,
Mark the self-evanescence of evil's excrescence,
Watch them feeding their mystics on juicy statistics,
Hear bliss roar through the craters of grain-elevators!

O this spirituality of pure externality!
Which can patch up disasters with arnica plasters,
Pipe the fountain of men's ills with cunning utensils,
Catch a shower of schisms in a cistern of isms!
Were the world one vast greenery of hot-house machinery,
Could you speed all creation with the spur of taxation,
Do you think that would muzzle the asp in the puzzle?
Would it snuff out the fire of the primal desire?

O dance of the dishes!   O pulse of the purses!
O whirlpool of wishes!   O chaos of curses!
O hybrid hypocrisy of high-bred democracy!

O self-contradictions of pious convictions!
O mental congestions of insoluble questions!
Are there no panaceas for a glut of ideas?
Here's a sweet little charmer who dotes upon karma!
Now why should it please her to worry and guess
Whether last she were Cæsar or merely Queen Bess?
We all came from Eve, and we're bound to confess
That her first incarnation was not a success.
Or, horrible thought! 't was perhaps a baboon,
Or a small elemental who fell from the moon!
For you never can tell when your head starts to twitch
If it means a Mahatma, or only a witch: —
Which accounts for reliance on Psychical Science.
Nay, take the bread pills of your hypnotized wills,
Even antidotes sweeter than the Baghavad Gita!
You may ride upon tables that mount to the gables,
Or hum the doxology in terms of astrology,
Or prove a prime gabble-er concerning the Kabbala: —
You may play with the derrick of things esoteric,
Or hear from a ghost by a note through the post: —
But, you'll find slight relief in eschewing roast-beef,
Or the juice of the berry that sparkles in sherry;
For be sure that the devil can find out your level
Be you common-place people or a-perch on a steeple.

O you West in the East, O you East in the West,
Were it best that you ceased, best at least for your rest?
For you're lost in endeavor, and tossed in commotion,
As the blood of a river on the flood of an ocean.

And you laugh like a bride in the season of June;
And you dance like a tide at the kiss of the moon.
For you leap like a pard from the rock-hidden throne
    of your pride;
And you plunge like a gull in the storm-ridden plumes
    of the main;
And you flash like a star from the sun-bidden voids of
    the spheres. —
But your plunging is vain,
And your leaping is wide,
And your flashing a moment of years.
For though in a whirl you pass by us
Like the rout of some fleeing Darius,
At length as of old you shall come
Out of this second pandemonium,
And kneel with the mild
Faith of a little child: —
Untangle the snarls of your skein,
Assort them and weave them again,
Massing all the reds
With appropriate threads,
The blues and the greens
In harmonious sheens,
Purples and yellows
At peace with their fellows.

Yet such chromatic powers
E'en now are dimly ours;
Foretaste of human bliss

In tuneful synthesis!
Music, our fairest, latest daughter,
Diamond of perfect water,
Plead for the West before the throne of Truth,
Pledge of our unripe youth!
Who spaced the vibrant stars
Of self-taught orchestras,
Breath polyphonic
From heavens harmonic,
The sympathetic nodes
Of Orphic odes?
The spirit of Beethoven
With worlds of unseen spirit woven,
Melody white with glee
Like yachts upon a sea!

Gemmed white with glee
Like yachts on a sea
When the blue waves sparkle to breezes free;
Or a-cool in calms
Of a pool of palms
In the sunset seas of the master, Brahms.

What shall we say
At dawn of day
To the lark that leaps from the lilac spray?
Would it not suit
The note of a flute
Afloat on the tremulous waves of a lute?

Or a murmur of breeze
Through the summering trees
Let the soft strings hum like the humming of bees;
Or a trumpet sweet,
Like a wing on the wheat,
As it flings ripe gold at the listener's feet.

In the first amaze
Of a West ablaze
The tone clouds glisten with scarlet rays,
While the inlaid whirls
Of roses and pearls
Are sweet as a chorus of laughing girls.

Like the crimson of plums
A long line comes
With the long-drawn sweep of the stirring drums,
And the answering rills
Of a thousand trills
Are filling the purple cups of the hills.

Now a rattle of hail
From the rising gale,
And the storm-clouds sweep like a world's torn sail!
And the piccolo's shriek
Is a lightning streak,
While the big bass booms as the thunders speak!

Now it sounds afar
Like the rush of a car,
And a moon caresses the evening star;

And a sweet smile lies
With a tear of surprise
On the quivering lash of the world's meek eyes.

Like spirits blown
From an astral zone
Are drifting the wonderful mists of tone.
And the moments seem
To drift with the stream
Till I know not whether I die or dream.

* * * * * * * *

"Let us mount! let us mount! 'T is the spur of the
      horn!"—
Let us stay! let us pray! 'T is the peace of the morn.

PART V.

The Future Union of East and West.

Yet once again discordant trumpets cease
To mar the music of the hemispheres.
So shall the future world a rose of peace
Blend with the tender lily of her prayers,
And music sweet shall float upon her airs
To melt all souls in floods of happy tears.

O wing of the Empress of mountains,
What song shall we draw from thy fountains?
Shall it come with a flutter of doves?
Shall it foam with the nestling of loves?
Shall it soothe with the poison of sleep,
Or dance like a sun on the deep?
Nay, no prattle of children or elf,
But the self-hood unconscious of self!

Soul of my inner face, face of my race,
The play is o'er. Remove thy tragic mask,
And show that hidden feature which no god
Hath e'er divined; till she, thy counterpart,

Bent o'er thy heart when listening to thy sleep.
Then in thine own true dream she saw thee smile
With sunlike manhood; and she said, "'T is well.
The world has waited.
With my kiss he wakes!"

* * * * * * * *

Breathe thy kiss on the world's twin soul,
Mornings that sleep in a crystal vision!
Waft thy music from pole to pole,
Airs that sweep from the fields Elysian;
Star-planes lighted by Love's transition!

Gaze, O world, at the sleeping sea
Perched on thy castle in fond amazement.
Open thy spirit to breezes free,
Open to whisper of love thy casement:
Fling it open from roof to basement.

Space is the kiss of the breeze's daughter;
Kiss her gently, and worlds are one.
Time but the flashing of restless water;
Ages are lost when the day is done
In the infinite now of the setting sun.

Let us forget like a chanted tune
Shadowy types of the dying races.
History nods to her ancient rune.
Ages lapse with their tidal traces,
Blend in the vision of future faces.

Fold like the wing of a new-born creature,
East and West in a Janus trance!
Tear off the mask of the twofold feature;
Kiss in the mirror with eyes askance,
Love, Narcissus, thine own sweet glance.

* * * * * * * *

God hath willed this soul to be
Like twin branches of a tree,
Whose wet leaves the sunset weaves
In one choral crown of glee.

Petals of infolded plan,
Model of millennial man,
Thine the vows of bride and spouse
Plighted since the world began.

Life shall be a twofold game; —
Harmony thy primal aim;
Individuality
Twin-born guerdon of thy fame.

What then shalt thou harmonize?
All that force the Westerns prize; —
Masculinity of measures,
Vigilance of Argus eyes.

Whence shall spring harmonic norms?
From the sun the Eastern warms; —

Loving femininity,
Fertile flower-bed of forms.

Then shall art with beauty rife
Melt into the Art of Life,
And the marts of industry
Win for starving sons of strife.

Stir of mill like hum of tabor
Singing of goodwill to neighbor,
Exaltation of creation,
Apotheosis of Labor!

If true harmony is prized,
Man is self-decentralized;
Christ's impersonality
World-absorbed and emphasized!

Not a crushing code of rules
For a paradise of fools;
But fresh joy of leaping fountains
Mid the broken shafts of schools.

Faith incredulous of creeds,
Love is full of bursting seeds;
Scatters showers of living flowers
Through a wilderness of weeds.

So may perfect Art and Prayer,
Life and Faith in union rare,

Build the soul new tabernacles,
World-encircling domes of air.

Age of worship crowned with spires,
Flames of purified desires,
Consecrate thy knights for battle
With thy symphony of choirs.

Who shall sing this song of spheres?
Whose the soul's baptismal tears?
Who anoint with tenderest touches
Christ's eternal wounds of spears?

Thine, O thine, that martyred breast,
White-souled Virgin of the West,
Heaven-crowned sisterhood of sorrows,
Love's incarnate Alkahest!

Who shall arm these knights with flame?
Who transmit the oath-bound aim?
Who shall crumble stars to powder
With the sceptre of God's name?

Thou, O selfless self-sworn priest,
Soul-wrapped manhood of the East!
Let thy heel with diamond lightning
Blast the eyelids of the Beast!

Fuse the worlds with inward light,
Faith-fed kingly anchorite!

Fire of Bodhisattwa Wisdom
With the Sun of Love unite!

Thus may knighthood of defiance
Consecrate the arm of science;
Twin-joined vigor of the ages,
Corner-stone of God's reliance.

Thus may Christlike Mercy render
Holiest warmth to Beauty tender;
Twin-joined womanhood of races,
Sunlike heart of God's own splendor.

Corner-stone and sunlike heart!
Strife in Wisdom, Love in Art!
Thou art joined in twofold marriage,
Links which Time can never part!

* * * * * * *

O unveiled bride,
Sweet other self at my side,
I ask no wedding bliss
Of passionate external kiss.
Let not the trembling pulse of lips
This purer ecstasy eclipse.
'T is not a palpitating form
I clasp to bosom warm.
I feel thee wrap my soul
As in the splendor of an aureole.

I breathe thy breath as through my spirit came
A tongue of Pentecostal flame.
No human spouse e'er felt
The culminating fire in which I melt.

   There let it burn
Like clouded incense from a temple urn;
And in its fragrant steam
Thy thoughts unfold like angels in a dream,
Unutterable things,
The fluttering music of elusive wings,
Flashings of interspacial laws
Wafted like webs of gauze,
Bathing the room
In floods of opalescent bloom!
And, as the dead arise
In transformed drapery to open skies,
When wreaths of petalled trumpets wrap the stars
In last triumphal chords of orchestras,
And in the stern archangels' tracks
The skies dissolve like fields of smoking wax; —
So from my inmost core
Shrivelled like paper in a furnace roar,
Or rocks where lavas hiss
From Ætna's treacherous abyss,
Rises a bloom of heavenly asphodel;
Bursting its elemental shell
A song of wingéd bliss
As from Creation's chrysalis —

A dim uncertain form divine,
O love, thy soul and mine,
Draped in soft veils of holiness,
Shrouded in Deity's caress!
Slowly it floats like spirit mist
By forests of tall tapers kissed,
Slowly alone
Up to the gilded altar's throne,
Hovering there
Like a condensing universe of prayer; —
Girt with bright-haloed constellations,
Memories of incarnations
Glowing like fallen leaves
Upon fresh-garnered sheaves.
There for a moment brief
It sits like God upon a lotus leaf;
The still unspoken Word
Before Creation stirred,
Or the transcendant Dove
Fell like a ray of love; —
Then fades in formless light
Too exquisite for human sight;
As when some saint is lifted up and hurled
Out of this mortal world,
This temple transitory
For Nature's unemancipated priest,
Into the silence of Nirwana's glory,
Where there is no more West and no more East.

MINOR POEMS.

PASTORAL.

'Neath the hill, beside the stream
    Stands a lowly shepherd's cot.
But contented doth he seem
    In his humble lot.

Seldom strays the traveller here.
    No one helps him sow and reap.
He, as our Redeemer dear,
    Loves to tend the sheep.

Fragrant is his simple life,
    Earthly sin to him unknown;
All his friends the flock and fife,
    Otherwise alone.

Innocent devoted one,
    Would my heart could be as thine!
Sweet the crown for service done.
    Lord, like his be mine!

DECEMBER.

The crafty wind
Doth now unbind
The giant of the winter blind.
With cold slow breath
A curse he saith,
And softly wraps the earth with death.

The hills make moan.
The birds are flown.
The leaves on barren graves are strewn.
Or hanging sere
They mock and leer, —
The charnel spirits of the year.

And thus we die.
Our hopes are high ; —
But Time shall turn his wintry sky.
O bliss ! O grief !
To be a leaf,
And flutter for a moment brief !

THE HOUR.

Soft the purple night is falling
    Over moor and dell.
Whispered prayers of love recalling,
    Chants the evening bell.

Cool the hour when dear ones hieing
    Seek a well-known spot,
There to one another sighing
    Of they know not what.

But the wood-thrush sighs and knows it
    Where the glow-worms peep,
And the drowsy west wind blows it
    Where the marsh buds sleep.

There on tiptoe moonlight listens
    To the cooing dove;
There the silent dew-drop glistens
    For my waiting love.

REQUIEM.

        Speak softly and low
Of the dead that are laid 'neath the willows asleep.
They have felt their last pain; they have dealt their
            last blow, —
        Tread softly and weep.

        No murmur or sigh
Comes up from the grave with a thrill or a shiver —
We listen in vain for a moan or a cry
        From over the river.

        But soon we shall tread
The path that they trod; and the mantle of sleep
Shall cover us all as it covers the dead. —
        Speak softly and weep!

THE DRYAD.

I wooed the gentle spirit from a tree,
And asked her, "What art thou that thou shouldst be
So patient in thy green eternity?

"Why dost thou brood upon the mountain lone,
Where mortal ne'er may hear thy plaintive moan,
Hear thy sweet sigh, and blend it with his own?"

She answered like a zephyr soft and low,
"The cause of my estate I do not know.
I live — am happy — God hath willed it so.

"Think not, proud soul, that all is planned for you.
Where men come not bloom flowers of fairest hue,
And Heaven unfolds the same ethereal blue."

ON OPENING AN ALBUM.

Your flowers are dead : — the fair sweet flowers
   You gave me in the days gone by.
Not all the cooling summer showers
   Could save them. They were born to die.

These roses on their withered stem
   Hang crushed and brown that bloomed so red.
How fragrant when you gathered them!
   And still their perfume is not fled.

No : — and the scented heliotrope,
   Blue-eyed and pure as maiden's breath,
Dear token of our love and hope,
   Lies faintly sweet though wan in death.

So like the flowers we droop! Like these
   The pink-veined hope of youth decays;
And maytimes from the apple trees
   Snow down dead sweets upon the ways.

Yet lingers in this vale of tears
   Some fragrance death may not remove;
Yea, from a spirit crushed with years
   One perfume sweet whose name is love.

So now to you, though far apart,
   In song like scented leaf, I pray,
O press these verses to your heart
   As you would me if I were they!

THE SOUL QUESTIONS.

The voice of the Present unheeded
   Is drowned in a tempest of sighs,
Those sighs that the fancy hath breeded.
   The Past is the beam in our eyes.
We look o'er a garden unweeded
   For rapture of bloom to arise.

Alas, for humanity's error,
   The self that bewilders the brain,
   The pleasure that whirls in the vein,
And brings on the phantoms of terror,
   The terrible demons of pain!

The cities are buried in gloom.
   The temple of man is a waste;
   A shaft on a desolate waste.
He laughs like a ghost in the tomb
   To which he is starred. In his haste
He prays for the curse of his doom
   As if it were gold of the graced.

On the beacon of hills is a breath,
   But a gasp, of the life-giving air,
As it flees from the rising mist, death,

That blows through the valleys its hair,
The thoughts of its pestilent hair;
And soft to the universe saith,
"Behold me, ye fools, and despair."

O God, if delusion is all,
If fancy and pleasure are cheating
And luring on man to his fall,
If beauty be fickle and fleeting,
If thought be the worm in the sweeting,
If truth be a loosely built wall
Where doubt like an ocean is beating: —

O, why didst Thou give us to be?
Not crush the dark seed of creation?
Why suffer each doomed constellation?
Why foam in thy querulous sea;
If all be not blessing from thee,
And crowned with thine utter salvation?

THE GOLDEN AGE.

This world was not
   As it now is seen.
It once was clothed
   With a deeper green;
And rarer gems
   Than the ice-caves hold
The sea brought up
   On the sands of gold.

But rust of ages,
   The breath of Time,
The meadows covered
   With early rime.
And the wild grass faded,
   The gems were gone,
And the wave fell cold
   As it thundered on.

In bygone ages
   The world was fair,
And the moon-god played
   With her golden hair;

THE GOLDEN AGE.

And the paling stars
   With love-white arms
Bent down to welcome
   A sister's charms.

The air lay sweet
   With the breath of pines,
The hill-tops glowed
   With their wealth of mines.
And sweet, and low,
   And rich, and free,
The wild dark music
   Stole over the sea.

And the sea-waves laughed
   At the saffron moon.
And the musk rose smiled
   With her soul of June.
And the golden age
   Of nature's years
No warning heard
   Of her coming tears.

But the hand of man
   Was the sword of death.
A poison lurked
   In his savage breath.

And the wealth of years
    And the glow of years
Were drowned in a flood
    Of swelling tears.

The world was fair
    In the days of yore ; —
But that golden age
    Shall come no more.
The sun may shine,
    And wild flowers bloom ; —
But the goal of all
    Is the open tomb ; —

The end of all
    Is the silent grave.
And beauty lies
    In the cold still wave.
And the world shall harden
    The hearts of men
Till it hear the voice
    Of its Christ again.

THE SNOWDROP.

Poor snowdrop, early for a snowdrop born;
The February sun is high, and winds
Steal from the feigning South with breath of spring. —
But frost-gods only hide. Sweet flower, they wait
To nip thee. See, snow crusts the fallow fields;
And yonder schoolboy cracks the thinning ice.
Behold what gloom of cloud hath chid the West.
Alas, I think I hear the cold wind sigh
In dread March days among the naked trees.
The woodman still doth fell the kitchen log;
And in his winter nest the squirrel hides.
I see no glad spring bird, save chick-a-dee,
Who bravely hops along the leafless bough.
Snowdrop, this night the North King's icy breath
Will blast thy budding hopes. Then, pretty flower,
I'll pluck thee from thy root; and thou shalt lie
Beside the one I love, and wake warm smiles
From her pale face at thought of me and thee.
The sight of thy young life may quicken her
To health and hope. Sweet silent messenger
Of love, I envy while I pity thee!
There: — tremblest in my hand, my hard rude hand?
Thou soon shalt lie upon her gentle breast;
And thou shalt die where I have prayed to die.

LOVE'S YOUTH.

O DELICATE harp of Love, from whose gold strings
   The poets and the gods have deigned to waken
That classic hymn which softly o'er me flings
   A fragrant dew from morning willows shaken

By Cupid's hand, these dreaming eyes shall praise
   The Fair whose sway decreed thy glad creation,
Who laughed to hear the eager boyish lays
   That woke thy heart with innocent elation,

When years were tranquil as an olive leaf
   By sunny Argive seas. A broken shaft
To-day we cherish in our shallow grief.
   We weep for thought of one who ever laughed.

Sing for me once again, and let thy waves
   Ripple upon my bosom as a beach.
Lend me thy notes that hushed the echoing caves;
   And calm the frenzied forests with thy speech.

Call up a strain of melody so sweet
   That broken hearts shall vibrate like a rod
Of mellow silver. Let the cadence beat,
   And die in wonder at the throne of God.

O harp of youthful Love! If these pure tones
   Be dumb forever, if no sunshine breathes
Through airs of passion, if thy lips in moans
Must turn to ashes in these clouded zones,
   Take back, O harp, my crown of laurel wreaths!

SONNET.

MY PERFECT TRUTH.

SHALL love my angel be? Or shall the flame
   Of wan ambition singe her tender wings?
   Why do I scoff at life to say deep things,
And crush my heart to yield a bloodless name?
If thou wert dead, O God! what bitter blame
   To yean these thoughts self-barbed with cruel stings!
   O let me nest near some warm soul that sings;
Not starve beneath a lone pale shaft of fame!
Yea, were I regent of the potent lore
   That lamps chaste sages' swoon, or crowned to see
The white-hot diamond secret at the core
   Of winnowed wealth of worlds that yearn to be; —
Then would I scorn these tempters o'er and o'er,
   And clasp my perfect truth in only thee.

SONNET.

MY SACRIFICE.

SEE how the Northern sky with gauzy green
   The pink pearl blushes of her bosom pales,
   And hides her nuns of stars with hasty veils,
Whose wanton eyes wink through the futile screen,
And sparkle kisses to the moon serene
   As through cool bays of blue he veers and sails
   To lift the rainbow lace in countless trails
That bar the chamber of his midnight queen.
So have I hid when fond desire my breast
   Hath stained to crimson. So I veil these sighs
Until some tear that will not be repressed
   Speaks through the quivering fringes of mine eyes. —
Then like a god thou comest from the West
   To sip the fragrance of my sacrifice.

SONNET.

FUJI AT SUNRISE.

STARTLING the cool gray depths of morning air
   She throws aside her counterpane of clouds,
   And stands half folded in her silken shrouds
With calm white breast and snowy shoulder bare.
High o'er her head a flush all pink and rare
   Thrills her with foregleam of an unknown bliss,
   A virgin pure who waits the bridal kiss,
Faint with expectant joy she fears to share.
Lo, now he comes, the dazzling prince of day!
   Flings his full glory o'er her radiant breast;
   Enfolds her to the rapture of his rest,
Transfigured in the throbbing of his ray.
O fly, my soul, where love's warm transports are;
And seek eternal bliss in yon pink kindling star!

SONNET.

HER LOVE.

I would thou wert a moon, and I thy cloud
    To wrap in rifted tangles of my tresses
    Thy soul's white naked mirror, lave caresses
Of soft pale pleading lips where thou art browed
With coronets of constellations proud
    Meet for thy regal thought; blue wildernesses
    Spreading eternal couch where love confesses
Her airy penetrations, where the shroud
Of my translucent bosom kindling gleams,
    Melted upon thy flame in blissful swoon,
Fused with the silver passion of thy dreams;
    Thy heart's strung harp a-throb with hidden tune
Winged from the primal pulse of God's own themes.
    O joy to be a cloud, and thou my moon!

REPROACH.

Pleasure has left me,
    Happiness gone.
Thou hast bereft me,
    I am alone.
Sweetly the summer night
    Heard thy farewell;
And the moon's tender light
    On thy face fell.

Thou hast betrayed me;
    Yet I forgive,
For thou hast made me
    Thine while I live.
Though my heart's broken,
    Take thou my last
Sorrowful token
    Due to the past.

If it be pleasure
    Brightens thy sun,
Let not its measure
    Lawlessly run.

Life hath her duties
   Stern and unchanged
Moulding her beauties
   Sadly estranged.

Think not, thou fair one,
   Love hath grown cold.
Still doth he bear one
   Thine as of old.
But I shall never
   Happiness see
Wedded forever
   Lyra, with thee.

Life has grown dreary
   Since thou art gone,
Lingering weary,
   Hopelessly on.
Ne'er will I blame thee,
   Ne'er till I die.
Slander may shame thee,
   Never will I.

Dull was my spirit
   To thy young breast
Fluttering near it,
   Dove, to thy nest.

REPROACH.

Was my emotion
  Sombre and cold?
Billow of ocean
  Hoary and old?

Jollity's glitter
  Dazzled thine eye,
Turned from the bitter
  Sweetness to try.
One you discover
  Fairer to see.
Never a lover
  Truer to thee.

Soon shall I moulder
  Deep in the grave,
Or in the colder
  Tomb of the wave.
Lyra, forget not
  Passion so true.
False one, regret not
  I bade thee adieu.

THE WOOD DOVE.

Gentle purple-throated dove
Nesting in the bamboo grove,
   Cooing, cooing, cooing;
I've a secret for you, dear.
Let me whisper in your ear.
Let no other creature hear;
   'T would be my undoing.

Tenderly pressed, pressed, pressed
Soft in your nest, nest, nest,
Carefully list, list, list,
If I be kissed, kissed, kissed,
If I be ——

There, you know my secret now,
You, too, on the topmost bough
   Wooing, wooing, wooing.
Did you tremble when he came?
Did you feel his lips a-flame?
But you shall not know his name;
   'T would be my undoing.

Tenderly pressed, pressed, pressed
Close to his breast, breast, breast,
Under your nest, nest, nest,
There shall I rest, rest, rest,
There shall I ——

SEPTEMBER.

The last light of summer hath faded and gone.
The sweet autumn days come enchantingly on.
The breasts of the trees don a joy-colored hue.
The sky is a curtain of mystical blue.

These airs, they caress like a maiden's soft hand.
The mountains lie purple, and misty, and grand.
And forests are mellow, and gardens sing gay;
And Nature is smiling this fair autumn day.

Goodbye to poor summer. No doubt she did good;
Though sentinel birches were scorched in the wood.
Her heart was too warm; but she meant to do well.
And we bade her goodbye as the mercury fell.

Hail, goddess of autumn, I see through the sky
Sweep on in the cloudlets resplendently by.
Thy form is half hid; but I know thou art there
By the sweet-scented breath which is borne in the air.

Come, apples and peaches, and fall from the trees.
And ripe yellow plums, tumble down at your ease.
And, clusters of grapes hanging blue on the vine,
Come down and be eaten, or pressed for pure wine.

SEPTEMBER.

O sweet the long lashes of sunny-eyed days.
Their bosoms are hid in the mantles of haze.
How cool is their mossy green lap in the shade
Of golden-haired oaks with their rock-maple braid.

O lordly September, thou prince of the hills,
The loyal green meadows grow gold with thy thrills.
The mellow sheaves fall for the harvesters blythe.
And I hear the sharp tinkle of whet on the scythe.

Let 's think not of days when this beauty shall pass,
And the splendor fade out from the hills and the grass,
When through the bare tree-tops the wind whistles shrill,
And the hoar frost at morning is white on the sill.

No, no. Torrid summer is over and gone.
The fair autumn days come enchantingly on.
Then bask in the sunshine, or sit in the shade
And watch the bright clouds as they color and fade.

NEW YEAR'S EVE, 1875.

Relentless Time, dear friends, has breathed again
His wintry mood o'er Nature and on men.
Long since the recreant sun's declining power
Has clipped the merry daylight hour by hour.
Long since the feathered tribes on tireless wing
Have sought the regions of perpetual spring.
Now bound in crystal chains the woodland lake
    And laughing streamlet hushed to silence lie.
Now earthward softly floats the glittering flake,
    And gathering storm-clouds drift across the sky.
Dead in the hollows lie the autumn leaves,
    And through the naked tree-tops softly stirs
The spirit of the dying Year, and grieves
    In slow, sad moaning to the Universe.

Not so man's soul. Than all the year beside
    Dearer his home is when the cold winds blow;
Great his domestic joy in winter tide,
    And bright his hearth as piles the drifting snow.
'T is then the happy children hail the day
    That Christ a little child like them was born.
'T is then the old are young, and young are gay
    With the felicities of New Year's morn.

We stand indeed 'twixt two eternities
    Of Time; and one has vanished like the dew.
    Deep in its breast the stellar systems grew;
And in its dead arms now the last sun lies.
A million ages drop from life and mind
    As yesterday, when they are past, and all
    The planets circle at their central call,
And never note the years they leave behind.
The slow earth cracked and shrank mid rains of fire,
    Till through the dull mephitic atmosphere
    Young Life arose, and whispered, "I am here!"
And thrilled the Universe with new desire.

Far in the sand a sculptured stone appears.
    Deep on the halls of kings has grown the mould.
    O, Love is ever young, and ever old;
And hand in hand with Time walk hates and fears.
Deep in the wondrous strata of the earth
    Bones of successive ages crystallized,
    Humanity lies only half-disguised.
A chipped flint tells us of a nation's birth.
From out the mother liquor of events
    Precipitates the dim historic tale.
    And thou, Old Year, hast passed within the vale,
And night shuts o'er thee with her spangled tents.

We stand upon the threshold of an ocean,
    And hear hard by the foaming waters break
O'er sunken reefs. We feel the wild commotion;
    And the salt wind leaves damp spray in its wake.

But like a magic curtain shuts the mist
    That open sea forever from our eyes,
Rich argosies that sail before the East,
    The infinite horizon of the skies.
Ho! Captain of yon bark, so stanch and brave!
    What noble aim has fortified your sail?
What guide-post have you on the trackless wave?
    And points your compass at the moral pole?
Peer long into unknown futurity!
    But shallow seas and rocks thou needst not fear
    When full equipped; for in that clouded sphere
Thy will alone is master of the sea.

'Twixt two eternities of Time we stand;
    But three infinities of Space.   Where lives
A human soul, in whatsoever land,
    Our heart to him a joyful greeting gives.
Yet on the wearied continents the bounds
    Of artificial custom wax and wane,
    As war drifts o'er them like a hurricane,
And death's hot hell unleashes all her hounds.
O, then we sadly find, with all our art,
    And scientific pride, and conscious boast,
    He falls the farthest who has climbed the most,
And man is but a savage yet at heart.
E'en as an earthquake comes unheralded,
    Or some volcano splits the trembling skies,
    We know not when the giant will arise,
And frighted earth be steeped in gory red.

Then things we held most dear shall pass away,
    And life be crushed beneath an iron spell,
    And earth shall groan, as when Atlantis fell,
And all creation dreamed of Judgment Day.

Poor France! Thou wast the first to feel the blow,
    Caught in the specious tyrant's silken net.
    Thou hast the ghost of Freedom only yet;
And in thy breast too many hot sparks glow.
Thy Teuton master stands with frowning brow
    Like Jove before the Titans. In his hands
    He holds the keys of Fate. To his commands
The trembling kings of earth reluctant bow.
An unread mystic obelisk he stands.
    But when his shadow on the dial falls,
    Grim shouts of death shall shake Valhalla's halls,
And pyramids be crumbled into sands.
Yet, like a crouching monster, in the East
    Slowly the Slavic power unfolds its coils;
    And effete Asia falls into its toils
A wounded bird, that can no more resist.
Or, like a tidal wave its course shall be
    Above the Aryan cradle of the world,
    Until, against the vast Himályas hurled,
To Heaven shall rise the spray of that wild sea.
Let Britain now usurp the old domain
    Of dread Sesostris and the Ptolemies,
And found that Eastern Empire, which in vain
    Napoleon dreamed of and designed for his.

Then face to face will meet the mighty foes
    For the death grapple. Saintly Pity's knell
    Will sound in shrieks. And in that lurid hell
A thousand years will melt away like snows.
As some great continental artery
    Empties its flood upon the coming tide,
    And in that grand collision far and wide
Tiptoe to Heaven stands up the frothing sea,
So shall the struggle of the nations be
    When flood-gates burst by press of passion high.
    The earth's wild wail shall plash against the sky,
Yea, shake the dwellers of the galaxy.
And can we, children of the Island race,
    Stand far aloof, like eagles in a cloud,
    And hear the rushing of the conflict loud
Like some dull echo off in shoreless space?
Nay, in the network of Atlantic coasts
    The ties of brotherhood too close are knit;
    And when the trial comes, prepared for it
America shall marshal all her hosts.

GOD'S FORESTS.

Let us give thanks for friendly solitudes
Of dark primeval woods,
Where jaded kings of men
As at a shrine may charge themselves again
With rays magnetic
Of fire prophetic,
Currents of inspiration
That circulate through God's unspoiled creation.

'T is well the human soul
Is nature's final goal;
That worlds dissolve in time's relentless void,
And suns should be destroyed
To yield one drop of penitential bliss,
Or the sweet perfume of Christ's pardoning kiss.

Yet flesh-spun bodies
Dim not the sphere where God is.
Nor are these care-worn streets the places
Where fall the gentlest dews of spiritual graces.
The fevered pulse of over-nourished wealth
Bodes not of health.
Nor is it Christian life
To glory in the elemental strife,

Inherited from birth,
'Twixt man and earth.
Or why
Boast of our eagerness to multiply
These sense-distracted strings,
That sound no newborn note of hopeful things,
But as in dreams
Babble the self-same themes?
O pity! that our toil
Sunk in this precious acreage of soil
Should feed, ere harvest day begins,
The wasting conflagration of our sins!
Better the unripe times
Of pregnant Tertiary climes
Where the slow-ebbing waters lay
Upon rich mines of vegetable clay!

Is there no flaw
In title of a self-consuming law?
Play we the tyrant less
In thin disguise of democratic dress?
Who gave the right
To disinherit man for revels of a night?
And am I free to desecrate my home,
As Nero burned his Rome?

God made the mountains lone
Crowned with the nimbus of a cooler zone
For evening worship of the weary plain;

And tilted up their sides
To give the impulse to His founts of rain;
And clothed them with His robe of living green,
And folded them in gauze of misty sheen,
As lovers deck their brides:
Full-orbed, and mellow in their juicy youth;
Not swept by sudden flood
Of hot intemperate blood,
Nor wan with limp distress
And quick exhausted by their bald excess;
But fresh and moist like ever vernal truth:
Yielding a sympathetic tear
For every crisis of the tragic year,
Saving earth's tidal flow
For daily bounty to the fields below,
Or spreading kindly wing of storm superb
To shield each parching herb,
Even as planes of unseen spirit brood
O'er thirsty deserts of our human mood.

Caught in their net of roots, as in a cloud,
The small drops slip
With many a sob and drip
Down the draped bosoms of the granite-browed;
Till with shy looks
Of fairies gliding from a hundred nooks
They leap together
In swift cool plashing of the hidden brooks.
Now bolder-hearted,

Skipping from dewy fringes of the heather,
As tears of joy escape in clearing weather
The soft lids parted,
Or children who should roam
Unconscious of their long deserted home,
So hand in hand,
A happy laughing band,
They dance upon the gardens of the land.

So shall the gladsome music of their bliss
Breathe life upon man's wearied industries.
No laggards they,
Or careless drones upon a wanton way,
But ever helpful in their lightest play.
Whether in moments still
Of dreamy mood on heaven-reflecting lawn,
Or racing like a startled fawn
At whistle of the mill,
Or in the frenzy of their maddest reels
Churning the curds of froth from circling wheels,
Or far, far down
Lightening with laughter of their lips
The stately march of heavy-laden ships
Toward the town; —
Gladly they water every hopeful soil
Of honest human toil,
Till blended with the elemental seas
God grants them well-earned peace.

So let us thank Him for these hills of pine,
The voice divine
That echoes in His plan
For self-bound man;
And from His purer ways
In nature's sweet unbroken peace
May we behold the law of our release
In life of thankful use and reverential praise.

LOVE AND MUSIC.

     God spoke!
His breath upon cold planes of space congealed,
Like morning's rising wreath of smoke
    Above a vernal field!

    It was the piercing Word
That the long shining coils of Chaos stirred!
It blossomed like a snowdrop from a frozen sod —
    The word was God!

Yet in the very bosom of this Law
    A blazing star I saw,
    Whose sympathetic glow
Melted the crystals of that universal snow
    Into one blinding human mood of thaw.
    It was the message of the Holy Dove,
        The unity of Love!

    So in our crowns of praise
Woven in soulful moments of our earthly days
I know the circling secret of a joy transcends
The ministry of thought for colder, clearer ends!

  Ah, Music, thine
The throbbing, bleeding, unifying heart
That burns within the central shrine
  Of perfect Art!

  And speech,— O, speech!—
Lies like a pure white maiden out of reach—
  Farther and farther down
  She circles like a falling crown.
  And from this sensitive and rare
Harp of the unarticulated air
A soft rose-scented cloud of beauty swells,
As from a myriad nodding fairy bells
  By breath of morning rung,
As if each ether-atom had a tongue.

  Ah, Music, tell us
Harmonious secrets that shall make speech jealous.
  Let poets crawl
Over the dusty mountains of yon ball!
  Let utmost fire of verses run
With hiss of rockets to the absorbing sun!
  They have no words
To match the spontaneous eloquence of birds.
  Their whispers vainly drift like trees
  Upon the torrents of the astral seas.

And when the Sun in moody frowns and smiles
  The universe inbreathes,
  Or shoots coronal wreaths

In maddening radiance through a million miles,
The master of the lyre alone shall hear that spell
Like some rapt maiden listening to a white reverber-
      ating shell.
    Thought leaps beyond
   The painful cycle of a finite bond,
   Swept to a hot magnetic plane,
Like smoke of burning worlds caught in a hurricane.

   So, Music, thine the deeper, truer word
   God in the temple of His silence heard
     When sense was born.
   No outward broken symbol angels knew.
   With one harmonious throb of Love they flew
Upon the pearly bosom of that primal morn.

AT HER TOMB.

The forests hang sober,
   The winds mutter dread.
They speak to my heart,
   But my heart it is dead.
Like breath of a spirit
   They sigh through the trees,
But my sorrow is deaf
   To the grief of the breeze.

Far off in the woodland
   Is dug a new grave.
My soul is there buried;
   No saviour to save!
There violets murmur
   A fragrant farewell;
And the cricket's low chanting
   Resounds through the dell.

I lie on my bosom,
   And sob to their sound;
My cheek in the grass,
   And my lips to the ground.

AT HER TOMB.

O hearts may be broken,
   And bitter tears come;
But the dead cannot hear thee.
   They sleep and are dumb.

Hang out thy red lantern
   O star in the East,
That the morning may break
   And my soul be released!
But the mist only hangs
   Thicker yet on the night;
And I hear a low sob
   As it stifles thy light.

Is it winds that I fancy
   Are lisping my name?
On the cross at her head
   Seems to burn a pale flame.
And a horror has seized me,
   A fear and a thrill,
That the souls of the buried
   Are nigh to us still.

Ah no, hollow chamber!
   Farewell, thou dear gleam!
'T was a fancy deranged
   By the lull of a dream.
But I call thee, and shudder,
   I writhe, and I moan
That thy spirit should vanish
   And leave me alone.

TELEPATHY.

O would we were downy white feathers,
   Or gossamer fabrics of laces,
To float through the stratum of weathers
   To the calm of the infinite spaces;
To linger like stars which the peaks at morn
   Compel to receive their caresses
On the low gray couch where the day is born,
   And wrapped in the gold of Aurora's tresses!
    O, whether the world be weary
     We'd care not a snap of a finger;
    You on Dhawalagiri,
     And I on Kunchinjinga.

On the breasts of the snowy Himályas
   Firm rounded in virginal fashion,
We'd burn like the crimson of dahlias
   At the twin pink foci of passion;
You with a rainbow arch beneath
   And the Milky Way to lie on,
With the Zodiac for a bridal wreath,
   And the diamond brooch of the great Orion.

Ah, whether the world be weary
    We 'd care not a snap of a finger;
You on Dhawalagiri,
    And I on Kunchinjinga.

Away from the curses and crazes
    And deserts of vulgar desire!
To know the impalpable mazes
    Are the exquisite centres of fire!
Where the spirit can doff the world's deceit,
    And stand in its naked glory,
And woo in the white of a native heat,
    And not in the vows of a lying story.
    There, whether the world be weary
        We 'd care not the snap of a finger;
    You on Dhawalagiri,
        And I on Kunchinjinga.

A fig for the standard ascetic!
    We 'd crave no intangible blisses.
On the ray of a current magnetic
    I could feel the throb of your kisses;
I could hold you close as a sweet pea vine
    With twisted tendrils a-quiver,
I could drink your breath as a spicy wine,
    As a thirsty desert absorbs a river.
    So, whether the world be weary
        We 'd care not a snap of a finger;
    You on Dhawalagiri,
        And I on Kunchinjinga.

Were not this the proof of divinity
    To love without limit or measure,
To raise to the bliss of infinity
    The Tantalus torture of pleasure?
For the new-blown rose of your cheek shall pale,
    And buds dry up with their juices.
But this fountain of youth shall never fail.
    The angels know its immortal uses.
        Come, whether the world be weary
            Let's care not a snap of a finger,
        You on Dhawalagiri,
            And I on Kunchinjinga.

REVERIE.

Where moonlight is stealing
Through juniper branches, I stand;
And my heart
Is wrapped in the feeling
That falls from some wonderful land
Where thou art.

I mirror thy sweetness
In fancy upon the blue heaven
Afar;
And sigh for the fleetness
Beside thee to float that is given
A star.

Cold mist like a spirit
Blown in from the East settles over
The sea.
Sweet music: — I hear it
Borne far from some wingéd sea-rover
To me.

Like hope in the distance,
To silver the sorrow of night
With her ray,

A ghostly existence
The beacon is glimmering bright
　　On the bay.

Yet little I reckon
Of music or moonlight redeeming
　　The sea;
Of starlight or beacon.
My loved one, I only am dreaming
　　Of thee.

IN THE AURA.

In the marble crypts of the clouds I would lay me to sleep.
Enwrapped in their foaming shrouds I would laugh, I would weep
At the floating dance of my soul like a buoyant feather,
Where far above in the fire-blue dome of the weather
Uptossed on the ample pools of its deep-dyed spaces
Would eddy the maple leaves of the passionate faces
Who kissed their hearts away in a burnt-out Past;
And ashen motives of deeds in a stare aghast
Upthrown to this world of shades from their astral tombs.
Like wreaths of a curling smoke shall their faint perfumes
Expand to the rarified hem of the atmosphere,
And play with its crystal balls; or in anguish peer
O'er the pale impalpable rim of their magnet globe,
As they cling with the clutch of fate like a thin silk robe
Round the maddening curve of its limb. And an angel star,
Shot down through the film from nebulous realms afar
To the central court of the sun, with a long lost fire,
Would swoon in the white hot tides of the mad desire

That reeks from the crust of earth, and his wing fade
    gray.
From my cold calm bier I would snatch at his robe, and
    pray:
"Dear ray of the cosmic grace like a pale Christ dying!
O mated dove of my soul in thy terror flying!
Come rest in the down of my nest till the world burns
    up,
And drink the draft of sin in her whirling cup
Till the soulless dance dies out for the lack of breath; —
For thought, and love, and pity shall outlive Death!"

SONG OF THE WIND.

Cheerily,
Merrily
Dancing along
The crest of my song
Breaks over the lines,
And foams as it reaches
The marvellous beaches
Of dark tossing pines.
Here I go rushing
Down into valleys
Half shadowed over;
Brooklets are hushing
Themselves in the clover
That laughs at my sallies.
Here
Like a deer
Let me race
On the prairies,
With dews for the flowers,
And diamonds in showers
To gem the blue face
Of the delicate fairies.
Down in the grass

SONG OF THE WIND.

Lightly I pass
Slipping,
Or dipping
As a wild bird
In the trough of a sea,
Or as a herd
When bushes are stirred
Merrily skipping
Over the lea.
Kiss me, you wild rose,
While I embrace.
Thou art a child, rose!
Why should the rush
Of a pink in a blush
Come over thy face?
Darling, but this is
The joy of thy kisses:—
That I may bear
Thy sweetness of breath
In a blast of fresh air
To a chamber of death.—
Ho! little swallow,
Let us both follow
Into the West
The car of Apollo
That rolls to its rest!—
Good-night, birch-tree,
Hie thee to sleep
Wrapped in thy leaves.

Why dost thou search, tree?
Why dost thou weep
Where the nightingale lingers?
Why wring thy white fingers
As a maiden who grieves? —
Here is a city.
The lamps are all lighted.
Poor folks are sighted
Only by me;
Shivering,
Quivering
Down by the corners,
Querulous mourners.
O what a pity
Such sadness to see! —
Out on the road again.
Down in the grassy lane,
There is a country lass
Milking her cows.
Plump are her arms.
Shall I arouse
Her love or alarms
By greeting her brows
With a kiss as I pass?
Ha! There's the moon
Reigning so lonely! —
Let the wench go;
She's in her teens. —
This is the only

Empress of night.
Better to know
The kisses of queens.
What do I care
For the wrath of the fair?
Must I bow to her light?
Shall I hush in a swoon
For this lady of air?
Nay:—cloudlets grasp her.
Stars try, but miss her.
Let me go kiss her.
I too will clasp her.—
Rogue of a star,
You queer little eye
Of an angel whose gaze
Is fixed in amaze
Over the sky;
Out with thy gleaming!
Wink now, and bellow,
And turn thyself yellow
To hear the blaspheming
Of such a bold fellow!—
Good-night, heaven!
Farewell, flowers!
The clerk of the hours
Is ringing eleven.
Earth, good-night!
May dreams of pearl
Weave starry numbers

SONG OF THE WIND.

Into thy slumbers,
Sweet young girl
In thy robe of white!
All things sleep.
Now to my rest,
Rocked on the breast
Where the wild songs creep
Of old nurse Ocean.
Soft be thy motion,
Wrinkled dame Deep!

THE CAPTIVE.

Have you seen a captive warbler in his gilded cage in May
  With his tiny bursting heart against the grating?
Have you set him where the shadows of the garden branches play,
  In whose silken bowers the busy birds are mating?
    On what joyous cradles of the giddy tossing crests
    Doth he mark them weave their nests!
How they chuckle and they snuggle with their little glossy breasts,
      Violet scents
Wafting shy delicious blessings to their leafy bridal tents!
      Ah, but he
Beats against the cruel mesh his shattered wing in agony;
  A wild melodic ecstasy of anguish utters;
  And like a flaming spirit flutters
    To be free.
And one tiny yellow maiden on a spray of lilac poises.
  From her little throbbing throat what luscious noises
    Warble love, and promise of a summer's bliss for him,
    Chirp a dainty kiss for him,
As she turns her pretty head askance with supple coquetry.

And will she never know the maddening fate that locks
    his cage?
Doth she not tremble at the elemental grandeur of his
    rage?
        Dear, sweet, unconscious brutes!
        Unhappy singers! —
But weep thou tears of blood, my heart, for distant phantom fingers
  Fore'er in vain outstretched to pluck thee from thy
    roots!

KARMA.

You never will give me the credit
   For half of the passion I feel.
My manner was cool when I said it.
   You mistook my refusal to kneel.
Well, the master of courtlier phrases
   You may have for a beck of your hand.
But I never shall sell you my praises,
   And I mean when I woo you — to stand.

What on earth is the use of a lover
   With rose-scented kerchief and breath?
Is he bagged like a bevy of plover?
   Will he swear to adore you till death?
Ah, till death! — He's a coward, my mistress!
   It is death he should first have defied!
Here I claim you through eons of histories
   Incarnate forever my bride!

Can you dimly remember, I wonder,
   On the tremulous breast of the Nile,
How once you committed a blunder?
   How your captain was won by a smile?

How you lay in a bower of spices,
    And maddened his eyes with your charms,
Till, praying forgiveness of Isis,
    He sank in your passionate arms?

Well, I clearly recall you at Florence, —
    'T was a cycle of centuries after, —
How you faced me with eye of abhorrence,
    How you stormed at the scorn of my laughter,
When you reckoned in impotent fashion
    I would welcome you back to my cottage;
You, who bartered a genuine passion
    For a mess of the ducal pottage!

O, I'm fickle? No doubt, since you know it!
    Each honey-sweet blossom to enter
Perhaps is becoming a poet,
    To revolve as a disc on its centre.
But the heart of a sphere has no motion.
    'T is an ultimate atom, serene
As the depths of a turbulent ocean. —
    That heart I reserve for my queen.

There, how would you like me to woo you?
    Shall I prate of the wonders of science?
Shall I come with a summons to sue you,
    Just to see your eyes sparkle defiance?
Shall I buy you an exquisite jewel?
    Shall I swear to obey your behest?
Shall I damn you as icy and cruel,
    Then weep like a fool on your breast?

No doubt you deserve all my damning!
   I only wish you would damn me,
And be done with this pitiful shamming.
   I would like you as fierce and as free
As a tigress, as supple and fearless,
   To dare you, and hold you, and shake you;
Or a Mexican mustang peerless. —
   I swear I would mount you, and break you!

Nay; I'll pluck you a star from its setting,
   And fling it with scorn at your feet.
I'll exasperate Mars with my fretting
   Till he lend you the glow of his heat.
Then I'll come like a double-ringed Saturn;
   And congeal you with polar embrace
Till you spit in your rage at the pattern
   My frost shall imprint on your face.

Ah, enough! For I dare you to sever
   That intricate fabric of meshes
You have woven for once and forever.
   No cycle of spirits or fleshes
Can stay that insidious leaven.
   It draws us like Fate to its level.
I will lie on your bosom in heaven; —
   Or, you'll go with me to the devil!

MAYA.

Where the willow meshes tremble
   On the bosom of the night;
And the fire-flies reassemble,
   And in happy dance delight
With their golden skein a-tangle
To deceive the stars that spangle,
Like a universe a-quiver,
All the surface of the river; —
Have I seen the subtle vision
   Of a strange unearthly thing
Peering forth as in derision,
And an eye as of a creature
   That was crouching for a spring.
Be it fiend or be it human,
I could feel each hidden feature
Had the semblance of a woman.

For I hear in sudden hushes
   Rustling like the sound of dresses,
And I see among the rushes
   Lines like tangled coils of tresses,
And I press upon my eyes
Where a veil of cobweb lies;

And my vision seems to dance
In the mazes of a trance,
And I tremble like a deer;
Is it love, or is it fear?
For the wind comes by and grieves
Through its harp of summer leaves.
Where it lifts the willow laces
Not a sign my fancy traces
Of the something that I dread
In the hollow of their bed; —
Then I pray it to appear,
When it answers with a leer;
And the leaves a-laughing shake
Like the ripples on a lake;
And it may be curse or kiss,
But I hear its mocking hiss.

Once I could not bear the passion
   Which it burned into my soul
   Like an eye of living coal.
And I cried to it with ashen
   Lips apart, and husky breath,
   "O thou messenger of death,
Cease this wily necromancy
Which has spun about my fancy
Like a web of cruel mesh
Chains that eat into my flesh!
O thou seraph, or thou fiend,
By thy boughs of willow screened,

I conjure thee to unveil.
In the sheen of moonlight pale
I must see thee, I must know
All thy hidden bliss or woe!"

Then a perfume as of musk
Seemed to permeate the dusk.
And I heard the willow whispers
Sighing like a nun at vespers,
Like a nun who knows her breath
Is as sweet as love and death.
And their leaflets seemed to linger
Like a soft caressing finger,
And they tempted me with tips
Of their passionate young lips.

Then their branches slowly parted,—
   In the blackness of their space
   Lay a dim uncertain face,
And its eyes were diamond-hearted.—
Then I heard a plash and scream
From the bosom of the stream,
And the vision paled almost
To the blankness of a ghost.
But I shrieked, "Thou shalt not go,
Thing of evil, child of woe!
See, the moon has half-way ploughed
Through the curtain of yon cloud —
She shall see thee, she shall tell
If thy message be from hell!"

Then a perfume sweeter, thicker,
Made the starlight faint and flicker;
And the dim uncertain feature
Took the semblance of a creature
That was beautiful and human.
For its breath came fast and warm,
Like a rising summer storm.
And its spirit turned to mine
For the madness of a second
Like the lighting on a pine.
And its pallid finger beckoned
Where the willows purred and pressed
On the lilies of its breast.
God! It was living woman.

Now the sap of spring a-bud
Leaped like fire in my blood;
And in broken voice I cried,
"O my gentle willow bride,
I have felt thee, I have known
That my soul was thine alone.
I have bartered hope of grace
For this vision of thy face.
Now the night-mist hardly dims
All the splendor of thy limbs,
All this witchery that swerves
With the passion of its curves!"

Then I saw no more, or cared;
For I threw myself possessed
On the marble of that breast: —
When I felt against my ear
Like a snake her icy cheek,
And the sting as of a jeer,
Half in sob and half in hissing;
And the moon came forth and stared
Like a white nun pitiful
At the beauty I had bared,
At the bosom I was kissing.—

O 't was horrible, my shriek!
I caressed an empty skull!
And the ripeness of those charms
Fell to ashes in my arms! —

Weeping willows, soft your plaint
Sweeps the moss whereon I faint.
River rushes, creep and crouch
O'er the madness of my couch.
Kiss and curse me once again.
I forsake the way of men!
Rock me sadly in the spell
Of your witchery of hell.
For, although I know the worst,
Still I love that thing accursed!

MAYTIME.

What are the small birds saying?
That I should go a-Maying?
"Ah May, May, May,
Sweet May, sweet May!
Do you love May?"
Thus they forever chirp in carol gay.
Prithee why should not I,
Marking their rapturous flight across the sky,
Echo to thee their spring-tide harmony?
Do I love May? Sweet birds,
A blessing for your sympathetic words!
Yea: more, far more than you or I can say.
Tell me, why is it that the name of June
Hath no such sweet associated tune?
Is it the hopeful play
Of possibilities in that coy "May"?
Perchance June's summer dust
Would soil the freshness of that "May" with "Must."
That's the mistake
We mortals ever make.
The shy wild-rose new-blown
We covet for our own;
And yet she droops when tied

To some dull stake, a limp defenceless bride.
No hot-house flower
Should share my true love's dower!
Give me the anxious thrill
That hangs upon an undetermined will!
Let May be ever "May,"
And in her girlish freedom laugh and play,
Nor doff the dainty mien
Of innocent sixteen.—
Then shall my pained heart flutter
Like a sweet bird with love it may not utter;
Nor know what blossoms hath
The gracious goddess showered in my path.
Ah, May dear, draw the curtain
Over thy smile uncertain.
For, be it tears that come,
My sorrow shall be dumb.—
Yet may I find
Perchance in some shy nook,
Betrayed of soft sweet-scented wind,
A violet by a brook;
Or one rare trembling white anemone
No other favored soul shall ever see.
No one but me
To catch in fairy dells
The tinkling of thy highland-lily bells,
Or watch the pure surprise
That shimmers in the blue-tipped grasses' eyes.
Shall I not press my cheek

Upon the daisies of thy fancy meek,
And let my soul be kissed
By furry, lithesome things,
The elemental spirits of the mist,
That float upon the dandelion's wings?
O May, if I should woo,
Not as a bee
With noisy minstrelsy,
If I should come to you
As comes a timid white-winged butterfly
Smiling to live, or smiling still to die,
What would you do? —
Nay sweet, haste not to tell.
I would not have you solve the mystic spell,
The pleasing riddle which the birds are singing,
In sweet reiteration ringing,
"O May, May, May,
Dost love me, May?"
Ah lack-a-day!
What is it I am saying?
I must be off if I would go a-Maying.

WITH DEATH.

When the lamplight dims in a mist of hymns,
And your sad, sweet glance in a glad trance swims,
When the tramp of the charging steeds is nigh,
And my pulse beats faint like a lullaby,
    And I know I must die:—
In that last sweet sigh, on that vast high brink,
Where the stainless fly and the sinful shrink,
What shall my innermost eye descry?
    What shall I think?

Shall the sad thoughts rush in a mad warm gush?
Shall they stand aghast in the chamber's hush?
And the ghosts of the past creep out and in,
Bone of my bone, and kin of my kin?
Shall I see you start with your first warm blush?
Shall I feel you smart like a wounded thrush?
Can I draw the dart? Can I heal you? Hush!
What is done is done; and the shadow of sin
Lies low with the sun; and they all troop in
    Pitiful visitors one by one.
Let them crowd to my bedside — let them come.
    They are mine; I shall face them, dumb.

When the flickering glimmer of the lamp grows dim-
    mer,
And the pale white lines of the curtain shimmer
Like a falling shroud, or a robe of cloud;
When I hear the snort of the chargers loud;
When a strong voice cries like a trumpet clear
"O soul, unveil; for at length I am here!"
With that last weak breath which the hand of Death
Shall snatch from my lip as he listeneth,
    What shall I cry, what shall reply
        When I know that I die?

Ah, this,— "Sweet bliss, I have lived, I have died for
    this.
I have dared thee, Death; I have sued for thy frosty
    kiss.
I have wooed thee in masterful mood; I have sworn to
    caress
My infinite bride in my spirit's first nakedness.
Out of the mists of my brain, and the storm of my
    pain,
Web of the flesh, and the mesh of the blood-swept vein!
Free like a feather to fly through the worlds as they
    crash!
I to be I evermore though they crumble to ash!
Never a wrath to fear: but a path to be won
Straight to the blinding light of a nightless sun!
Whether He cast me to hell, or fell me to earth;
Whether of sin I be shriven, or driven again to rebirth;

Ill is the slave of the will! I shall master it still.
Love shall not kill, though I drink to the fill of its ill.
Nothing shall daunt me: — not taunt of the damned as
    they chant.
Only weak purpose to fear, and the cold pale fears as
    they haunt.
This is the self-made sting; this is the cursed thing: —
To mutter the palsied doubt, to flutter with listless wing,
To creep like an icy snake in the grass of a sordid
    thought;
Never a passion to sin for, never a bliss to be fought,
Never a hell to be welcomed! — Then come to me,
    Death, though I burn.
Flames shall be quenched in our love, and God, He
    shall feel how we yearn,
And Mother Mary shall sit like a queen mild-eyed,
And wash the foam from my lips, my merciful bride; —
For gladly She loved Her Beloved, and sadly She loved
    till He died."

SPRING BREATH.

Like secret emerald sheens that hide in the froth of a wave,
So reincarnate greens from the drifts of their wintry grave
Have felt the breath of a spring as sweet as the pulsing blood
When a maiden plumes her wing, and love swells red in the bud.
The snows shall melt like a cloud, and their ghosts come back in the rain;
And the mountains thunder-browed shall frown on the timid plain.
But the feet of the shy blue maids that hide in the withered leaves
Shall bathe in the brooks of the glades, and dance in the mossy eaves
Of friendly giant rocks with their wonderful blurred gray eyes;
And the curls of the soft fern locks unfold to the kiss of the skies.
And down where a smoke-like smell lies low in the atmosphere
Is heard the song of a bell with the tinkle of silver clear

From the cool wet sponge of a shade; and the mouth of a shy pink cup,
Like a naked child afraid, for a draught of the dew looks up.
O rare anemone, like a pale pearl shell from a stream,
With the grace of a maiden free, and a firm green wing like a dream
Of the clustered emerald sprays round the new-born gem of a soul; —
See now through the crystal grays where the heart of an oriole
Hath drowned its orange throbs in the mirror soul of the brook;
And with sympathetic sobs the frightened violets look
Aghast at the sight of blood. But fear is as fragrant as death,
And fairies faint at the flood of this delicate maiden breath.
And the squirrel rubs his eyes, and scans the world from his chinks;
And the mottled wild duck flies from the sly gray lair of the lynx.

IN NORWAY.

Soul of my fathers,
Soul of black mountains,
Soul of gnarled forests,
Soul of hoarse trumpets,
Soul of world-thunder; —
Soul, be the fissure
   Rent for my gaze!

Thence shall I ponder
Midnights of revel,
Wolves of gray hunger,
Flames of salvation's
Martyrdom, triumph,
Churns of mad struggle,
   Curses of love.

These are my birthright; —
Here in the northland
Crags of the ice-gods;
Nest of gaunt heroes;
Cradle of sea-hounds,
Serpents of vikings,
   Doves of the skalds.

IN NORWAY.

Still doth the North Sea
Hurl on the granite
Helms of thy headlands
Barbs of white thunder.
Still through the blue wave
Dip the gray petrels,
   Sea-gulls of ships.

Into thy caverns
Hollowed in mountains
Breathless I wander; —
Frosty with jewelled
Drops of the moonlight,
Ghostly with echoes,
   Turquoise their floor.

Sprays of Aurora
Blaze to the ceiling.
Brackets of jasper
Hold the steel arches,
Rafters of crimson,
Tiles of green lightning,
   Studs of gold stars.

Harpstrings of sagas
Weird in your passion,
Pulsing with luminous
Snarls of the demons,

Faint with caressing
Breath of white maidens,
   Pure in your prayers! —

You have your power still.
Still do I hear you
Shriek your shrill voices
In the death-grapple,
In the ice cracking,
In the sea moaning,
   In the ghosts' cries.

Nurse of the rime-frost;
Gray sky and misty
Skirt of wild she-gods,
They that beheld me
Borne to my cradle
Like a young eagle
   From their hoar nests! —

Thou hast an infinite
Thirst in thy bosom;
Blood for the daring,
Glimpse of vast values
Toppling for heroes,
Whirls of mad kisses,
   Wombs of dark life.

O when the thunder
Crumbles old mountains'
Craggy gray castles;
O when the lightning
Stabs her red war-blades
Through thy ripe bosom
    Shrinking like curds; —

Then do I know him
Tyrant of Titans,
Thor the god-conqueror,
Twisting the iron
Dome of the elements,
Hurling hot satellites
    Chained to his glove.

Yea, and he sweepeth
Far to the southward,
Whirling cloud-castles
Down the horizon,
Lit like a rumbling
Crater of ruin
    Lost in the sea: —

While to the zenith
Frosty and quiet
Tips of sharp diamonds
Shatter pale lances,

Shoals of thin nebulæ
Froth with the beakers
   Of their star-wine.

Halls of the North-dawn
Crusted with garnets,
Sardon, and beryl! —
Into blood-ruby
Foam thy green goblets,
Trail through wan purple
   Pearls of milk-blue. —

   *   *   *   *

Hence with these visions: —
Meteor glances
Split by the icy
Spar of the present!
Fling them like dew-drops
Into the ocean,
   Whither ye flee!

THE DISCOVERY OF AMERICA.

A SYMPHONIC POEM.

THE DISCOVERY OF AMERICA.

A SYMPHONIC POEM.

FIRST MOVEMENT.

The Sea and the Sky.

BLAST of disruption triumphant! Wail of the travail of
    Time!
Shudder of terrified worlds in the glare of the sun of
    the new!
Thrills of the joy of creation! Potence of prophets
    sublime!
Faces in dust to be lifted, and crowned with the stars
    of the true!

    Crowns of the stars like wreaths
      On the lap of the midnight sky.
    And the sympathetic ocean breathes
      With the swell of a smothered sigh.
    Stars like the fallen leaves
      That in autumn die,

On the lap of the sea as it heaves
    With a death-foreboding cry.
But angels glorious, deathless,
Gaze from the windows of heaven breathless
    On bird-like ships that are floating by.

"O mocking, sighing, treacherous sea,
Whisper thy fathomless secret to me."

    Then the coo
    Of a soft wind blew,
And a shiver ran up to the flag at the masthead high;
And the blast of disruption blew, and the night wailed loud in her pain,
And the stars hid under a cloud that was heavy and blue with rain.
    And the small waves writhed as they came,
    Writhed like the wreaths of a flame,
    Like the luminous, drifting breath
    Of a wraith in the chamber of death;
    And their pleadings fell
    With the moans of a petalled shell,
    As they curled with purrings and hisses
    Their warm lips bubbling with kisses,
    Rolling in tremulous eagerness
    Of an amorous siren's soft caress
    For this second Ulysses.

But he cried in his agony,
"Away with thy cursèd lips, O sea!
And thy snaky fingers of weeds
That reach from the sleeve of thy frothing beads!
Echo no more the voice
Of our weakening spirit's choice!
Heaven knows that we yearn
For the secret impossible bliss of return.
But the flame of an inward fire
Burns fiercer than tenderest heart's desire,
A fire that feeds
On the very anguish of wonderful deeds.
Begone, I say! Make way, make way,
In the name of the Lord!
With His cross on my sword,
I carve from this doubt and temptation
A path through thy sheer desolation!"

Then the balm
Of a perfect calm
Fell over the passionate seas;
A fragrant calm
Like the hush of a psalm,
That hangs on the boughs of the cocoanut trees,
That hides in the heart of a great cool palm,
Where the coral harps like bended moons
Echo forever the splendid tunes
That float on the dreams of the broad lagoons.

Then the flying fish
Arose, and sped with a sudden dash
Like the shivering line of a lightning flash,
And sank again with a joyous plash;
Like golden shuttles in silver mesh,
Like love that leaps to the burning flesh;
Again and again, like the throb of a fresh young wish.

O wish that no god may know!
O throb of despair and delay!
O sob of another dying day!
O faith that flies like shaft from a bow,
Then sinks again in the floods of woe!

Then cried he in deeper pain: —
"O last faint flutter of hope, thou shalt not fail!
Breathe, breathe again
Into the pallid cheek of my despondent sail
The shell-hued glinting of thy gleeful gale!
Respond, respond,
O holy universal Mother of the seas beyond!
O brooding Dove, breathe inspiration fair;
Be it through lightnings of the summer air
That kisses warm
With furious fevered breath,
Or be it in the utmost throes of tropic storm;
Even in Death,
Reveal, reveal thy form!"

Hark!
A sudden shriek in the dark!
A whistle that shoots to the peak!
A darkness that sweeps to the deck!
A crash like a wreck!
O blast of disruption triumphant! O wail of the travail
of Time!
And the backs of the green waves break;
And the stout beams crackle and creak;
And the keels roll weak,
And reel in the cavernous wake
Of a violet lightning streak.
Shudder of terrified worlds in the glare of the lightning
sublime!

Shuddering rumble of thunder drums!
Wailing flutes of the hurricane!
Trailing beards of the matted rain!
Suns that crumble in blinding crumbs!

Hist!
Whistling from water-snakes' nests,
Pestiferous,
Vociferous!
Sulphurous gulfs!
Rushing of selfless elfs!
Restless cresting of helpless breasts!
Shifting rifts of the hapless mist!

And ever the shrouded form
Of the great gaunt god of the storm,
With eyes as of skulls
That shine in the lulls,
And fingers with skin like a wing,
That cling to the hair
With the clutch of despair,
As foul sea-claws to a drowned corpse cling!

O blast of disruption, and utter diremption!
O shudder of doubt that is passing the bonds of dimension!
O mental and physical tension
Of terrified worlds that are hurled as if lost to redemption!
Disruption! Distortion!
Destruction! Abortion!
Worry, and murmur, and motion of scurrying currents!
Tearing, and perilous tossing of turbulent torrents!
Murderous horror, and crossing of error with terror!
Scoff of the physical surf like a breath on the psychical mirror!
Mist-driven broods of the ocean like moods of our mystical nature!
Railing and blare in the tempest, and wail and despairing of travail!
Thrills of creation in glare of the wills of the powers of evil!
Swords that shall leap with the hour to the hearts of creator and creature!

"Ah peace, peace!
Santa Maria, peace!
Let the wild torture of this fury cease!
Yea, on this watery desert have I fasted, and sung thy praise
A thousand times over a Lenten season of forty nights and days.
Unmoved on the lofty tower of thy purposes dim I stood.
Lust, and Ambition, and Doubt, and Fear swept by in a hurricane brood.
But I was not, I am not strong.
How long, O Mother of our Lord, how long
Shall I be hammered as molten steel in the forge of this scourger's mood?"

O first unwelcomed foreigner!
O last unconscious mariner!
See, through the swift unravelling fringe of the shattered clouds
Light breaks.
Fragments of mist are swirling like lost bewildered flakes.
The stars are swimming in scattered crowds.
Tossed on the breast of heaven what waif is this from the wreck?
What messenger of hope alights upon thy shrouds?
A small brown speck
Helpless it falls, it flutters to the deck.

O thrill of a prophecy dying! O flutter of wingéd
    wish!
  "Nay; — 't is only a flying fish
      Hapless thrown up
  From the lip of the ocean's frothing cup."
"O comrade mine, what is 't? What is 't? — It
    stirred!
It cannot be — Jesu beloved, dare I lisp the word? —
    It cannot be, I say, —
    Great God, make way!
    A small land bird!"

  There it lies with heart a-tremble,
    Plumage torn by fire and hail;
  While earth's boldest sons assemble
    Weeping o'er its body frail: —
  Even as angel choirs are weeping
    Round some stricken tortured soul
  Freed from storms of sin, and sleeping
    At its last unconscious goal.

So flies the blesséd dove with olive bough
  To thee, lone wanderer on a world-wide ark.
So shall the smile of God direct thy prow
  To some new Ararat across the dark.
    Thence shall thine eyes behold again the sight
    That flashed on Moses from Mount Pisgah's height.
  Look up, for soon shall break upon thy brow
    What Israel's chieftain led, a pillar of fire by night.

How calm and how sweet the night!
   How fresh and how pure the sea!
And the cool salt air like a thing of delight
Sweeps over the soul as a wing in flight,
And the sky is barred by the caging bright
   Where hope is beating her plume to be free.
Thrills of the joy of creation in potence of prophecy
     new!
   And the stars new washed like a crown of leaves
     Are held in the arms of the virgin sky,
   Are raised by the royal love that heaves
   The loyal heart of the tiptoe wave
   At the new-found kiss of a master brave,
     Of her true-found prince who is sailing by.
Heroes on high to be lifted, and crowned with the stars
     of the true!—
        Yes, the true,—
        And the new,—
   Lapped by two great infinities of blue;
   Wrapped in the vapors of the cosmic dew.

     O thrill of the joy of creation!
     O will of the mood of devotion!
     O prophecy potent of ocean!
     O stars of the crown of salvation!
Penitent lifting of faces to infinite graces!
Permanent drifting of planets to ultimate places!

Potency patent of dust on the brow of the just!
Latent devotion of trust to the new she embraces!

But hark!
What was spoken?
Was it the throb of yon spark
That cuts like a Damascene blade to the dome of the dark?
Has the heart of a white star broken?
Was it the whisper of distance? Was it the blinding roar
Of wedges of light that are splitting the sky to the ocean's floor;
Even as solid edges of proud Vesuvius split
In the rage of a lava-fit,
When the glorious crimson blood spurts through with a hiss
The red ripe wound of each orifice?

O pillars of light that are lifting the glare of the glorified ceiling,
O fierce arabesques of the stars as they leap in antiphonal passion,
O shaft of the uttermost steeple that reels with the madness of feeling,
Here shower thy blazing cathedral on the corpse of this universe ashen!
Rise in thy architectonic splendor of radiant fires
From the womb of creative desires!

On the combing wave of thy crystal dome now set
    The diamond jet
  Of each sparkling minaret,
Pouring like infinite golden foam from the torches of molten spires!
    Let each tongue of flame
    Have an individual name,
      A voice effervescent,
        Evanescent,
Swept from the floor to the roof in a pæan incessant;
    As of luminous souls
    In the joy of their self-won force,
  Each on the tremulous wedge of a rocket's course
From the vortices shot of the duplicate cosmic poles!

    What gossamer network of comets' tails
      Shrouds heaven in rainbow veils!
Pulsing in changeable gold on the breast of this astral chameleon,
Filaments scattered like crowns of enamel on walls of Alhambra,
Orbital laces of loops on the centres of darker penumbra,
Flashing of manes from the chargers in star-clustered perihelion!

    Yet these soft skeins of astral floss
    Waving like beards of incandescent moss
      Of a sudden condense

By some centripetal master influence.
    Earth's breath is held,
As when in the gloomy slime of chaotic eld
    The atoms huddled in blank amaze
      At the soul-searching gaze
        Of the first created sun.
  So now, on this altar of night
  Blazes anew that sacramental light
    For a day's work done.
    Four-armed it lies,
A blinding prophecy in the central skies;
      A cross!

    How calm the night! How free
      After this meteoric ecstasy!
        The world is still
  With fixity of faith, and deep untroubled will: —
    Faith in the infinite blue spirit of the sky,
    Will in the infinite true bosom of the sea.
Purposes unclouded, and the goal like a star set firm;
Time but a gentle bride in Creation's fond embrace.
Kiss of a hero who lifts the veil from a virgin's face!
Goddess-birth from the foam of the sea at the God-
    appointed term!

      Ah, hero, weep —
  In the happy dreams of thy sleep,
Pillowed on folds of rosy-hued idea

On the deck of the Santa Maria.
Sail on, and dream
In the molten glow of this steady tidal stream
That bears thee sure
To worlds more wonderful and pure
Than thou canst deem.

And now on the tossing edges of the East
A higher wave of molten silver flashes,
Flashes a moment, and dashes
Like spray by the stars to be kissed.
Nay, nay,
'T is not wave-mist.
'T is a star that thou hast not seen;
For it flashes keen
With a diamond light increased,
And it comes to stay.
'T is a wave,— 't is a star,— 't is an arch,—
'T is the chord of a harp a-tune.
It wafts thee a secret thy fancy hath never heard.
'T is a luminous golden orb with expanding wing.
It shakes the sea from its breast as a king-like bird.
'T is the saintly, impersonal moon.
As a godlike thing
With solemn and dignified motion
She rises,— she leaps,— she is free.
She soars away on the constellated march
Of the deathless Zodiac.
Her parting smile irradiates the ocean.

It lies in the foaming wake of thy perilous track.
It beckons thee onward, not back,
'T is thy pillar of fire by night.
And so, with her virginal kiss on thy brow,
Slumber thou,
Dream thou now
Of the ultimate Light!

SECOND MOVEMENT.

Dreams.

O PEARLY themes that flutter like beams of the moons,
O languid dreams that swoon in the arms of the noons,
Like perfumes of blossoms that toss on the roses of bosoms,
Like spice-winds that pillow their sighs in the tresses of willow!
Like a passionate prayer from the lips, like a star from eclipse
Roll into the peace of the soul as a liquid diamond slips
Down cool green lotus leaves to the flame of the budding tips!
As their ruby hearts unfold to the warm noon gold,
Shell within shell unrolled, like a secret told
By a virgin bride without fear in a lover's ear; —
So, themes of his delicate dreams, expand in gleams
Of glorified visions that twine as a garland of vine;
Thought that shall leap from a thought as flame from a name,
Rays that are written on Time as a blaze that came,
As a blinding blast that shot from the womb of the past,
And pierced like a peerless star through the future far; —

Death in the bloom, like a child that shall dance on a
    tomb; —
Faith that hath kissed the blue mist in the dome of the
    vast.

    But see, he hath plunged in its sphere
As a joyful boy in the cool green floods of a mere.
His soul is light as the wings of a dragon-fly
        That leisurely dances by.

He stands by the dark gray gates of a city now;
And over the wreath of smoke that fringes the brow
Where castles cling like an oak to the crumbling crag,
Mid rumble of distant drums and the thunder of guns
He marks with a breathless hope where the sudden light-
    ning runs
        Of a Christian flag; —
Flag that hath leaped from its faith, as a flame from a
    name.
O imperial name that is written in deathless flame!

    Hark, 't is the drums! and a dark line comes
    With a trumpet peal o'er a wave of steel;
    Where the heroes march in a wide blue arch,
    And the chargers prance in a stately dance.
    Each knight sits light with his thin steel lance
    Mid banners in lanes of the ribboned manes;
    And strict in time to the martial chime
    A loud hymn reigns o'er the proud glad plains.

"I see afar the blaze of the jewelled tents
    In circling zones,
    And in the midst twin thrones
Like new-born stars on the startled firmaments."

   Hark to the fife, like a thin keen knife
   That cuts steel ranks on the Genil's banks
   For a queen set light on a charger white.
   In a deep black band the turbaned stand,
   And bow to the sweep of her lifted hand;
   While the stern chiefs come like Titans dumb
   To the low sad tap of the Moorish drum,
   That her glove may seize on the world's gold keys.

   "In this vast camp of Spain
Where plumes of knights are tossing like a crested
       main,
And coronets of swords shall leap with diamond tip,
   And forests of bowed heads shall dip
   At curse or smile on royal Isabella's lip,
I come to grasp the silken tangles of the rein.
       Ah, not in vain
       These years of cold disdain!
       I would have choked my pride.
For one sweet smile I would have crouched and died.
       But now all glorified
   She reigns the mistress of the universes wide;
       And I shall kneel, and cry: —
   'O gracious lady who hast bid me die,

The Lord divine
Now consecrates me for His own and thine.'

"Still cold and dumb?
I hear the heart-beat of a muffled drum,
The wailing of a dirge for heroes dead.
And dust is on my head!

"O blinding blast from the open tomb of the past!
Would that again I could rest on my mother's breast!
Would I could lie where the strife of these years should
   die,
And innocent kneel in the spells of the village bells!

"And yet I knew; and yet I dimly guessed
   When as a guileless boy
I climbed the steep Ligurian cliffs in lusty joy,
   And gazed far off upon the dimpled breast
   Of blue-eyed seas that slumbered in the West.
      For was I not compelled
      As by a great hand held
      To gaze, and gaze, and gaze
   Through tender brooding miles of purple haze,
      Till soft-winged isles
Seemed lifting orange bosoms to the sun's last smiles,
   And my light will, a feather free,
Was blown like a trembling bird far out to sea
By storm-winds, Alpine-brewed, of passionate proph-
   ecy?

"When calling to the straying goats
    That scrape and browse
Where silver-coated olive groves in sunshine drowse,
    Or climb in bleating flocks
For verdant vales that smile among the splintered rocks,
    I heard strange notes
Whispered in siren tones from distant dancing boats.
    At first in fear I hid.
Then, as in trance, not knowing what I did,
I snatched the iron cross from my panting breast;
    That cross my mother hung
To keep me ever innocent and young.
It clung to me as if it were a hand that tenderly caressed.
    But with one parting, burning kiss
I stood, and flung it to the ether's vast abyss.
    Far down I marked it like a circling flame
    Sink sunlike in the wave.
'O God!' I cried, 'whose sweet torn martyred frame
    Thy Virgin Mother gave
The fierce relentless worlds to pacify and save,
    I'll follow Thee,
Thou Master who canst walk upon the sea!
    Whether from pole to pole
    Thou lead'st my consecrated soul;
Be it to jungle heats of tropic noons that tell
    Of the despair of hell,
    Or to the caps of Hyperborean ice
That crush a starving world in hardening crests of vice,
    Or where vast silent lands like unexpected grace

May glorify the timid ocean's face,
   Be it for gain or loss,
      I'll follow thee
   Into that unknown sea,
      My Cross!'

      "Ah, then I felt
      A darkness like a belt
Drawn close around me as in ecstasy I knelt.
      And a slow disappointing chill
Like torture crept to the heart of my yearning will.
      And then I knew, as now,
      That I must die as Thou
      On crumbling naked plains
   Outside the city walls where ignorance reigns;
Alone, misunderstood, despised, condemned, in chains."

Death in new bloom, like a child that shall dance on a
   tomb!
Ah, cross of my doom, let me die with my Lord in the
   gloom!
Yet, Faith, thou hast kissed the blue mist in the dome
   of the vast.
O, fall like a peerless star that is clear to the last!

   * * * * * * * *

"But now for the daring of deeds! — Where these des-
   olate piles
Of rat-haunted, moss-planted wharves are complaining
   for miles;

Where the blanched and decrepit old salt like a ghost lingers still
With his tales of the glory of eld, till he pales at his story of ill;
Where the mighty façades of old Genoa painted like skies
Are but trappings that deck a dead bride on the strand where she lies; —
I can view like a seer, I can feel as a soul with new senses
The East beating in as a spice-laden breeze that condenses,
Where the forests of masts bear the fruit of the opulent marts,
And ships are like girls at a fair, and the world all ablaze with her arts,
And the scar-smitten men are like Argonauts newly returned
With the foam of the sea on their lips, and the blood in their veins as it burned. —
But visages turbaned and dark, and scimetars curved like a moon
Have swept with their Turcoman wrack as a storm on a hidden lagoon.
And the heroes and ships are no more; and the story of yore
Is heard in the streets like the echo of surf on a shore.

"But, my Lord!
O my drowning, my crucified Lord!
That this torrent of devils abhorred
Should dishonor the shrine of Thy grave!
What is gold, what is art, what is fame
In the curse of this shame to Thy name?
With Thy summons to save
I could rush through the world like a breath of avenging flame;
I would dare the vile monsters of seas where a ship never strayed;
I would carve me a way through the void with my blood on my blade
In the stress of that blessèd crusade!

"But, behold!
There is need of the gold
To bid for the charter of kings, and to mellow the hearts of the cold. —
Through the sea! Through the paths of the sea! —
And hath He not beckoned me on to a mission untold? —
Through the sea to the West! — Can it be? —
Through the West to the East! — O my God, through the darkness to Thee!
Where the roofs are ablaze with the wealth Thou hast stored for my fee!
Where even the Khan in his tents shall hail me with bend of the knee!

And the rays of the midnight sun behold like a pageant
  unrolled
Where the curtains of time are upfurled o'er the stage of
  a unified world!

"O themes of my passionate dreams, expand in the gleams
Of these glorified visions that whirl like a cloud in a
  pearl,
Where thought follows thought as a flame that shall swirl
  from a flame,
As a prophecy written on time, as a burning star for an
  aim,
Thy Star of the East that hath shot from the tomb of the
  past,
And pierced like a lance through the bar of the ocean
  far,
And sent me my faith like a star in the dome of the
  future vast!—

* * * * * * * *

"O, but how slow is time! How cold, how slow
My white-haired tides of effort ebb and flow!
How like a baffled mist I flutter to and fro!
  With restless questionings
I chase the mocking phantoms of my kings.
  With straining eye
I trace on endless maps the outlines of my misery.
  What gain to me
To follow hollow-eyed the shifting contour of the sea?—
  Not to the South

Where foam the heated tides from Niger's mouth
    I 'd steer these foolish ships. —
        My needle dips
Forever to the West where fancy slips
      Down endless planetary slopes,
And in the bitter sea of disappointment gropes
      The wreckage of my hopes.

    "Yet once, when near the pole,
      A strange aurora stole
Over the frosty darkness of my soul.
      On Thule's strands
Where Hekla like a priestess lifts gray hands
Out of the crystal tent in which she stands,
      A wondrous thing
      I heard a poet sing
Of islands in the West where blooms perpetual Spring,
      Where suns at midnight shine
      O'er vales of golden vine,
And gods and heroes press the nectar of their wine. —
      O for that liquid gold ! —
But now the juicy body of my will grows old.
    The vines and veins of hope run deathly cold.
I think the evening bell of my lost faith hath tolled.

    "Ah, toll, sweet bell !
      Toll, toll

Forever as a balm to some excruciated soul;
Sweet bell, whose surges swell
Like dancing lights upon the waters of a stagnant dell,
Like visions of a saint in penitential cell!
Toll
Well
Where surges roll
In a dirge's knell!
Read as a creed from a scroll
The secrets thy sobbings tell!
Roll
To the uttermost steadfast pole
Of a Christian martyr's goal!
Swell
As the cold white mornings stole,
As the shivering sunlight fell
When the Christ was vainly mocked by the litanies of hell!
Bell
Toll,
Swell,
Roll,
It is well
For the soul!
Now high to the roof fling the spears of thy leaping spell!
Now low at the base of the tomb lay the fears and the years of our dole! —

"But, fierce as a river that scoffs at the bondage of chains,
And proud as the ghost of a cloud that rides over the
 plains,
I mock at thee, bells; at the shock of your insolent yells.
I crave no relief. Let me quaff to the full of my grief!
Let me clasp her and kiss her, my sorrow, and laugh at
 her sting!
Like a knife let her cut to my life! Let my parted lips
 cling
To the darling keen edge of the sword of Despair, and
 be wrapped in her hair!—

"O bell, like a passionate prayer, like a star from eclipse,
Like the dancing of lights in the misty white marsh of a
 dell,
  Toll, toll, sweet bell, and roll
O'er the peace of the world, as a liquid diamond slips
Down cool green leaves to the blood of these foaming
 lips!
  Read as a screed from a scroll
  The secrets thy throbbings tell,
  Like a sobbing saint in his cell;
Shell within shell inrolled, like a sin untold
By a penitent maid in the fear of a master's ear!—
Lips for the knife, though it cut to the heart of my life!—
Faith that hath kissed the sweet strife like the tears of a
 star through the mist!

"O Faith! Faith! Faith! O thou soul which art freed from a wraith!
Though the body lie cold, and the bells of thy dirge be tolled,
Upspringing, outwinging, with a joy like a skylark singing;
Spurning the mourning, the scourge of calamity scorning,
Hearing but wedding-bells ringing, and burning with light of the morning,
Breathing sweet perfumes of blossoms that cross on the meekness of bosoms,
Proud as the prance of a steed that rides over a cloud!
I cling like a waif of the sea to the skirt of thy shroud,
Like a sailor a-sea in the surf to a rock that is browed
By the sad white smile of a dove as she flies to her love; —
Like a dove as she flies to the breast of her God in the skies;
Like a love as it lies in the depths of two beautiful eyes: —
To my Faith let me rise! Let me leap to the star of my prize! —
On this altar of light where the tapers are burning all night,
And the pillars of shades lie about in the dark colonnades,
Where the sense with sweet savor is dim, and the silence lies pure like a hymn,

I shall vow to Thee, bountiful Christ, like a prince of
    the blood I shall shower
The wealth of the world on Thy tomb, and the bloom of
    my strength for Thy dower!

"O Faith, my soul is swept in thy whirling clasp,
And twined with the spiral flame of a distant bell
Into some vast new plane of pure white thought. I
    grasp
Earth's crystal secrets, crowns of thorns in many a
    martyr's cell.
And naked facts, like startled souls at the trump of
    doom,
  Leaving their body of tangled lies in the tomb,
     Gaze at me earnestly face to face
       In this far cool focus of space.
      Suns turn, and spurn, and burn
  Like sacred jewels each set in a silver urn.
     .   Stars whirl and swirl
In their pathway of diamond-powdered pearl;
Each planet lifting her dainty aural robes
     From the trailing dust of the globes
With the swift wide-skirted swing of a joyful dancing
    girl.
       Across blue oceans of Nothing
  Currents of pale magnetic rivers are seething and
    frothing;
       Thought, like a soul-spun gauze
          Of cometary laws,

Weaving eternal bands,
As the flush on the cheek of the cold North maid expands,
Without hurry or pause.
And cool, and far,
And still,
Seated like Fate in a fixed gold car,
Somewhere in the nebulous wake of the polar star,
With His little finger that pulls as a primal will
God sweeps the orderly skeins
Of the cobweb reins
That hold the worlds in the netted leash of inexorable chains; —
And every wingéd mote like a needle speeds to those silent lanes.

"And Earth,
Dear, sweet, round, hornéd cup of the waxing Earth,
Blessed as the focal choice of the Christ for birth,
An open book thou art spread;
Each deed of thine a potent prophecy writ large in red;
Each second a seed of infinite fruit or weed that shall spread and spread;
Each soul a trickling dainty theme self-sung on a timid reed,
Until the heart-burst of its melody is freed
Into the wild chromatic rush of a symphony overhead!
And thou, dark slippery slope of a sea unstable
That would, if it could, obliterate
The encausted record-stroke of Fate;

Thou foolish flirt, whom the strong true core of this ball
    holds firm
    To the bed of an endless hymeneal term,
The numbered arcs of thy bond are graven as if on a
    silver table!

"O Christ, how every dotted island teems
With the potent agonizing bliss of Thy dying dreams!
    All far-blown faces, and races, and spaces
Are merged like drops in the omnipresent sea of Thy
    luminous graces:—
Dwarfed Ethiopians who dare the furnace of sand-
    choked wind,
And dark soft-spoken ruby-merchants from the templed
    rivers of Ind,
And moon-bosomed languid Arabian girls that sigh for a
    kiss as they play
In broken notes like a sob on the zither at close of
    day,
And yellow fur-clad gentlemen that hawk with the tented
    Khan,
    Or in fish-scale armor covetous scan
The blue of the rifted sea that hides the gold-towered
    roofs of Japan;—
        All these,
  And as many more as the shrunken earth may please,
    Thine anointed Admiral shall seize,
And lead to the tomb-throned capital of Thy Monarchy
    of Man!

"O pray, pray, pray,
Thou sobbing cathedral bell with thy tones of earth's sombre gray,
Now shot with the throbbing of bursting stars, now dark with the doom of dismay!
I kneel in the gloom of the flickering wax, and the saints on the altars sway;
And the shadows creep with the promise of sleep. — But thy clarion cries 'Away!'
I leap to my feet with a sword in thy beat; and the cold white kiss of the day
Slips in through a door like a ghost on the floor. — The friars are coming to pray.
O pray, pray, pray,
Dear peaceful golden souls enwrapped in the hood of earth's sombre gray,
Whose tidal dreams of bridal themes breathe love in a fleshless ray!
My passion blends with God's pure ends,
Where prayer like a folded air ascends.

"Peace, infinite, deep,
Lies in the arms of Resignation, like a babe asleep.
'T is not these earthly prayers alone.
I hear sweet choirs who hymn pure bliss at the foot of the throne."

O glorious themes of their faith like the crimson of lotus blossoms!
O pure white petals of folded hands on the crystal mirrors of bosoms!
O priceless pearls from their lips! O flames from their finger-tips!
Roll over the face of his soul as a diamond tear-drop slips: —
Prayer within prayer unrolled, as the word God told
Of eternal love in the dear sweet shell of the Virgin's ear!
Roll into the peace of the world, as the soft gray dawn that stole
Round the crucified Saviour's head, and sang as an Easter aureole,
When the faces of angels came, and smiled, and kissed the pang from His soul!

THIRD MOVEMENT.

Wedding Music.

      If in melody
    Pure truth were spoken,
     If on harps of glee
All dark-eyed falling rays to shimmering stars were broken,
       Then were things
       Flames with wings
Lightly in one another floating, as a skylark sings.
      Yes, each ripe morn
     Blown from a silver horn
Would wreathe itself in harmony of love for souls new born;
      Each heart-drop sorrow-drawn
        Would melt
     As crystal flute-notes felt
In pulse of dove-like flight o'er buoyant symphonies of dawn.

     So star-browed angels fly
    On wings of echoing notes
To some far Alpine call of a hero's horn that floats
    Down blue-lit corridors of sky;

Fly in wide sympathetic rings, and pause, and hark
To the new-strung chorded rim of the ocean's arc
Where three white ships like breathless swallows are skimming by.

   As when moons
  Through flooded heaven
  Trail trumpet-petalled tunes
In silver tendrils o'er the diamond trellis of the astral seven,
   So this flight
   Of a tragic night
Flashes a radiant message to the farthest nebulæ of light;—
   Yea, unseen spheres
  Sweeps in its song of years
For crested choral hosts aflame with their organ-pipes of spears,
   Spears of auroral rose
    That quiver
   Like sunsets on a river,
Or the crimson-hearted song that bursts when a lotus blossom blows.

   O listening silver sphere,
    What do you hear
When the round blue shell of the universe is curled at your ear?

What have the comets done
To the lips of the sun?
What whispers
Of penitent meek lispers
Steal to your far confessional like the sigh of a dove-eyed
nun?

Low bells
Now twinkle through the sky like stars from dimpled
wells.
Fair white-winged maidens stand
Who fling the trailing gauze of their torches wide
O'er the delicate fern-like limbs of a virgin land,
Of an innocent dreaming bride.
O, unkissed cheek of a moon that the pillows of spaces
hide!
O golden tresses of autumn leaves outspread!
O spicy breeze that sighs from a maiden heart,
They smile as they beckon a strange white prince to part
The foaming lace of thy bed.

Dear patient bride of Time,
For thee the unborn planets dream they chime;
As Orphic melody
That floats upon an unsuspected harmony;
As a babe's eye uncloses
In wonder at a waving mystery of clustered roses;

As if sighs
Of sense first won in losing Paradise!

   As if stars
  With hearts were throbbing,
   As if silver bars
In quivering minor melody of love were sobbing,
    So the curve
   Where white ships swerve
Sweeps with a tremulous moon-edged kiss to the lips of
  a naked nerve;
   And startled miles
  Dreaming of love's strange smiles
With a shiver twang the emerald harp of their thousand
  isles;—
   And bridal torches burn
    Like eyes
   O'er jewelled lawns of skies
Where laughing angels dance as light as the tiptoe dew
  on a fern.

   O dance as light
   As a fawn, sweet night!
  And let the starlight bring
The echo of the melody you sing.

   The liquid metre
     Of wind-swept pearl
    Where cloud-nymphs bathe
   In an upland tarn

Is clear as the ripple
  Of nights that swathe
The rounded limbs
  Of a white moon-girl.

Sweet as the twitter
  Of Pleiad swallows
  That build gold nests
In the purple eaves,
The placid hours
  With dove-like breasts
Their love are cooing
  In dark cool hollows.

And nebulous milk
  Of blue-veined skies
  That feeds twin orbs
In the lap of dawn
Is pure as the fire
  The soul absorbs
From the love-lit font
  Of the virgin's eyes.

  Ah, hero, drink thy fill
Of the fiery breath of God's will!
    Upon thine ears
      Converge
Through whispering galleries of the years
    The murmurs of the surge

Where swooning lipless voices
    Clamor for rebirth.
    Like a waked god rejoices
This captain of yon caravel of earth.
He leaps upon the rainbow bridge of hope, and scans far
    seas
    Through star-lensed mysteries.
        No spirit realm
    Is stranger to his helm.
        The peal
        Of his trumpet cry
        Cuts like a keel
            Upon Eternity.

Bring scarlet lilies
    That wander breathless
    O'er Martian meadows
In fluted fire!
And kneel in the hush
    Of Lunar shadows;
And spin gold crowns
    For a hero deathless!

Where leaping shuttles
    Of meteors pattern
    The pale brocade
Of the astral film
Now tangle his hair
    With diamond braid,

  And twine his fingers
    With rings of Saturn!

  And soft as feathers
    Of suns that hover
   O'er milky waters
  Where star-maids hide,
  Now bare your bosoms,
   Uranian daughters,
  To pillow the brow
    Of your sleeping lover!

So shall we set him on a polar throne,
And lay his hand upon earth's loosened zone.—
   O bliss
    Of a martyr's wedding-kiss!
Hath not each Christ who whispers down the years
Seen triumph blurred through halo-crowns of tears?
As if a truth-swept burning glass should melt
With the concentrated agony it felt?
O agony of tears, now blessed as wine!
Immortals drink thee with a sob divine.
And Bodhisattwa, clad with tainted flesh,
Crowned with the sting of blood-warm sins that mesh
Their diamond-hearted wills, o'ertop the world.
Like unseen germs in pulp of fruit-cells curled
Their thoughts swell rooted in the brains of kings.
The very heavens are stirring with their wings
Of rosy-hued idea. The Easts and Wests

Are held in their two hands; and on their breasts
Lie child-eyed prophecies of faiths and creeds;
And new-born worlds are twined like crystal symphonies
of beads.

Ah, play on the sorted reeds
Of plaintive years that slip
Like yearning beads
Of deep unutterable prayer
From a holy lip!
And dance
O'er crystal slabs of air
As light as the gossamer trip
Of million-footed Chance!

Come, play on the flutes
Of tempered eons!
Come, dance on the pebbles
Of time-worn suns!
Let young moons pipe
With their silver trebles!
Let comets prance
To the earth's proud pæans!

Shoot hymns of lightning,
O maids with torches,
Through unploughed tracks
Where the planets race!

Bow down, ye Lords
    Of the Zodiacs,
While thunder rolls
    Through your pillared porches!

To the silken tent
    The bridegroom flashes
  As a star-kiss throbs
In the earth's warm breath.
Now close it with curtains
    Of silver sobs;
And pin it with diamonds
    That slip from your lashes! —

O sweet veiled virgin land that lies like a leaf
  In the cup of the seas, in the lap of the drifting skies,
Drink softly thy draught of dreams, for the night is brief,
  For the cool still touch of the morn on thy shoulder lies!
Lay bare the bud-like founts of thy bridal grief!
Like a widowed nun with tears thou shalt wash the pearls of thine eyes.

As a tragedy leaps from its germ of deed, when a star
  Is born of the clash of suns in a fate-swept path,
So souls like steeds are spurred by the gilded car

To the plunging doom of their death, or in foaming
    wrath
Are whirled by the charioteer in a circle far
Down haggard face-browed lanes of a hero's after-
    math.—

    Must the liquid metre break
      On a storm-swept lake?
    And mar with its wailing bitter
      The Pleiads' placid twitter?
  Shall not the hero's diamond-hearted will
      O'ertop all ill?
    Then let the piping eons
    Dance to the earth's proud pæans!
    For if in trailing tunes
Heaven shall vibrate to the pang of new-born moons,
    If discord only strengthens
  The Titan-hearted harmony it lengthens,
    Shall not these blood-notes quiver
As if a million ruby blossoms floated on a tranquil river?

    As if some new melodic sense
      Were born of senses;
    As if the sun-burst of omniscience
Were shot from the seven-hued ray that a crystal soul
    condenses;
      So an immortal ear
    The pure white truth shall hear

As if it filtered through a soundless, formless, stainless
    atmosphere.
        How can it race
        O'er broken strings of place,
For everywhere is omnipresent in one burning focal point
    of space?
        How can it rhyme
        O'er rhythmic lapse of time,
For God hath swept etherial pulses into one limpid lake
    of love sublime?
As bubbling springs where tear-eyed nymphs have rule,
    The soul wells up with insight clear and cool.
        Each diamond-hearted brother
        Shoots rays into another;
And all things lie about on one another's breast like lotus
    petals in a pool.

    So the pure motive of the bridegroom speeds
As if an opal bird had dropped to an emerald nest of
    reeds.

        But what if he bear the sting
        Of a mortal thing,
And bind with the silken chain of a self the bride's
    unconscious wing?
What if he stain with a tear the virgin lace of her
    bed? —

Ah, Psyche, thy bed is the vast white ocean of human
   suffering;
And his the awful kiss of a soul with its own true free-
   dom wed!

When out of the calm cool gray of the primal night
         God's thoughts, breathed light,
Like clouds on the pearly wing of the morning flew,
         No sense-refracted ray,
No tear-stained dream of a separate self they knew.
         Like babes they lay,
Or folded petals asleep in the soft white arms of a dew.

         As tender flocks of tune
      Carol upon symphonic interludes of glee;
         As if a single dimpled moon
Showered a million diamond kisses on the crescents of
   the sea;
         So in a nesting mood
         Shall selfless spirits brood,
Cooing to one another in the ecstasy of dove-like
   brotherhood.
         To stand upon the brink!
         In crystal depths to sink
      Where saints in clear community of purpose think!
         Not as a mere drop lost;
         But as a new note tossed
      Into the overwhelming organ-floods of Pentecost!

O white baptismal font of impersonal fire!
    We dip in thee
Our helpless naked individuality,
And fling our separate beaded wills like pearls on a funeral pyre!

    He who seeks
    Shall find; —
Whether on mountain peaks,
    Or in the desert wind;
Whether with white dumb hands he shrieks
    To the future deaf and blind;
Whether on wasted knee bespeaks
    The lonely God of his mind.

    But where shall the soul aghast
Woo its true self in fierce immortal agony of passion?
Upon what deserts of the haggard crowd, in what gray garb of penitential fashion
Shall it invoke the purity of its long-forgotten past?

    Bathed in the sweet virginity
Of this young land that rises like a shell-nymph from the sea
    Behold, O man, the perfect crisis of thy opportunity!
    By bitter balm of conflict purified,
Alone shalt thou be worthy of thy starry bride.

Not as the lawless denizen of Greed;
But as the loving citizen self-freed
Pouring his life-stream into the ocean of the common
 need.
O fertile prophecies that laugh on a wedding morn!
O dispensation newly born!
For thee the systems waited, for thee the planets
 floated
Like smoke-wreaths ruby-noted
From the molten core of Time outblown through the
 lips of his silver horn.

If on wing of melody
The past reborn came flying;
If in burst of prophecy
The future sang its heart out in one note, like a skylark
 dying;
And if the sweet-lipped themes
Of these twin sister streams
Were pressed into the single rosy petal of an angel's
 dreams;—
Then the whole fronded world
Into this downy seedling moment furled
Would sing to itself, like God before one gossamer
 thought uncurled.
So, night without a parallel,
Sing on, sing well,
As with the bursting heart of Nature prisoned in thy
 sapphire shell!

As if the very blisses of the bride
Were charged with all the motherhood of ages to be
    crucified!
    As if the bridegroom heard
      The pinion of a Dove
Whirring amid the boundless transports of his love,
And brooding with the very impregnation of the Primal
      Word!

      O bridal night
Veiled in thy spirit robe of white!
      O panting wave
Of sea-green goddess in a glassy cave!
      O sky atune!
    O perfect-breasted moon
Cold with the splendor of a marble slave!
O braided stars upon the brow of Dawn!
      And Pleiads' nests
    Under the purple Wests!
And dove-eyed Lyra brooding on the lawn !
    And thy keen sword, Orion!
    And thou, O sun-tamed Lion!
  And thou, again, great polar heart
That pinn'st the wingéd universe's spiral chart!—
    All ye, and millions more
That teem in violet life upon the farthest astral shore!
  Whirr up in one transcendent blast of wings;
  And fill the jasmine melody that swings

From the pale yellow of magnetic stems,
And flings the cup-like magic of its hems
O'er the soft naked wilderness of things! —
Now in one last ecstatic canticle, ye moments, blend,
That mote-like rush upon the flaming end;
One perfect note of wedding bells to rise and sink
Upon the drum-like brink
Of steel-blue corded hemispheres,
Where now the mortal signal of the years
Is sounded for the fainting, dying world in elegies of
tears!

FOURTH MOVEMENT.

Triumph.

Hark! From afar elemental voices prophesying!
 Hist! 'T is the tune of the sirens of the deep!
Mark where yon star to an altar-flame is magnifying!
 List to the moon like a sibyl in her sleep!
    Hark through the mist,
        List
For a shiver like a wind upon a glassy river!
    List through the dark,
        Hark
For a rattle like the omen of a coming battle!
        Mark
      Where the spark
     Of a trumpet like a lark
Cuts against the dawny flashing of the dark!
        List
    While the murmur of the mist
        Dies away; —
  Dies away in the sobbing of the spray,
Of the spray of silver falling on a pool of amethyst!

Who waits
With calm white bosom veiled beyond the gates,
Where long cool chords of braided sleep
Trail with their stifled dooms upon the deep?
A breathless hush of wonder
Listens for avalanches of the muffled thunder.
Some blood-stained conqueror kneels awhile to weep.

"Sleep, midnight pure.
I hang this harp, my heart, within the spiral void of
thy delay.
The ministrel of the dawn is sure.
'T is sweet to pray.
How often have I prayed the night away,
Slipping on keels of eager glances into the silent onset
of the gray!

"How calm to velvet lips the moonlight nestles,
As if a Lilliputian fleet of silver vessels
Were spreading nautilus sails to mermaids' breath!
How the hushed drowsy zephyr dreams, and listens
To catch the beaded sleep that on the fringe of mid-
night glistens!
And the whole sea is pulseless with the poppy-ecstasy of
death! —

"But what is it glares and swirls with a trumpet-clarion
plume from the helmeted vortex of space?"

"Naught but the breaking moon on the mast!"
"A blinding golden Christ out-burst like a furnace-
    bloom from the womb of yon rifted place!
        Didst thou not see?"
"Only the swerve of a prow that ploughs to the furrowy
    edge of the vast;
        A shadow that wings to the lee!"

Hark! From afar elemental whispers penetrating!
   Hist! 'T is the croon of the yearning of the sea!
Mark where yon star with a diamond kiss is scintillating!
   List to the moon like a mermaid in the lee!

            "O wild suspense!
        O spasm of ecstasy intense!
        O agonizing moment like a knife!
    Was it the mortal steel-keen edge of an earthly light?
            Was it? — I'd give my life
        Did it not curse with the mocking glare of a hell-
            born sprite!"
    "Nay; it could be but the blade-like hair of the
        moon out-streaming."
            "O cruel, cruel dreaming!

    "'T is now the very breathless dead of the night.
        The moon hath set in the track
        Of a wingéd goblin black.

> The breeze is light.
> No sound to trouble
> The ear, but a silver bubble,
> A rounded hope that breaks
> In hollow aches!—

"But what is it puffs like a swift pale passionate lip in
the half-furled sail on the great cross-tree?"
    Hark! 'T is the prayer of an altar-flame afloat!
"O Christ-like voice of a Judgment lightning-bell that
shook wild orbs from the heart of the sea!"
    "'T is a star!"—"'T is a light afloat like a tossing
boat!
It flickers as fire-flies weave their ominous golden gleams
with the braided grasses!"—
    "Steady!— It glimmers!— It passes
As if like a luminous snake it glided through trees that
shrank on a distant shore!"—
    "Blank heaven! 'T is drowned once more!—
Again it lives!— It swims!— It swerves like a lantern
that waves on a strand!—
    O bursting prophecy of the ages grand!
It thrills to my soul! It throbs like a living flame in
my hand!—
    'T is land! 'T is land!—

"O star of salvation! O blessed exhalation!
O ecstasy boundless! O frenzy of forces!

'T is the flame of the land! Let its fierce exultation
  Prance up through the blood like a legion of horses!
Come, leap from your slumber, ye argonauts splendid!
  To your knees on the deck! On your wings to the shrouds!
Burn rockets of triumph for martyrdoms ended!
  And waft your white prayers like a dove to the clouds!

"The heavens are melting;— they swoon in their gladness.
  The womb of great Nature is bursting with blisses!
O helmsman, thou Anak, stand firm through thy madness!
  O comrades, embrace me, I pant for your kisses!
Flash lights to the Niña! Shout horns to the Pinta!
  O Martin Alonzo! immortals together
We have shared the cold scorn, we have dared the dark winter.
  I crown thee, my brother, with stars of spring weather!

"The past is forgotten. A truce to all rancor!
  I bless ye, dear children, who weep as ye kneel.—
Now leap to the windlass! Uncoil the great anchor!
  Stanch hopes of the dawn, how ye throb through the keel!

Here are crowns for our toil! Here is balm for all
 doubting!
 'T was the Virgin who flew with Her wings on our
 masts!
I hear the far blessing of cherubim shouting.
 Let them shake the thin walls of the sky with their
 blasts!"

O blast of disruption triumphant! O wail of the travail
 of ages!
O shudder and shamble of planets a-tremble with doom
 as it rumbles!
Cold dews of the new are upon thee; the curse of the
 blood of the sages!
The world splits apart with a crash, and the dome of the
 elements tumbles!
And onsets of steeded archangels have torn up the tents
 of old orders!
And pillars of nations dissolve in the breath of the ram-
 pant marauders!
And quakings have swallowed the sun! And the core of
 the universe crumbles!

And curses, like shrieks of a Dawn when typhoons from
 their ambush of Caliban lair
Have streaked a black clutch of demoniac claw through
 the pale shredded gold of her hair,

And, tearing pearl mantles to tatters, have snatched the
    nude pink of the manacled nymph,
And stifled the sobs of her swoon in the drowning sea-
    bloods of her own native lymph ; —
So curses of dark swollen crisis outburst counter-blasts
    to the challenge of morn.
So pæans of triumph swept back in a curdled recoil
    through the jaws of her horn.
And impotent engines of time fanned the terrified air with
    recalcitrant wing,
Like daring black plumes of a crow crested back by the
    hurricane hails of a Spring. —
Till, shot from the uttermost angle of space, blazed the
    rocket-like star of the Master ;
And legions of light through the infinite corn-fields of suns
    leaping faster and faster
Swept down through the shaft of the visible void with the
    crash of triumphant disaster ! —
And though worlds lay in stratified wreck on the beaches
    of systems, and perilous sheens
Of the crystalline levels of sprays spurted o'er the thin
    hulls of these Spanish marines,
Yet the hymn of the purpose of God, pulsing bliss through
    their hearts like a balm, was as oil
On this turbulent tide of their fate, and set finger of calm
    on the lips of turmoil. —
And the black ruffled plumes of the morn settled back on
    her pearly soft neck all a-quiver. —
And something sailed out from the rim of the sea like the
    ghost of a swan on a river. —

O hark to the hiss of yon spark, as it cuts with a Damascene kiss to the dome of the dark !
O list to the treacherous tune of the sirens that swim to the mystical whim of the moon !
O wait at the gate of the gray !
O kneel as ye reel to the sibilant sobbing of spray !
O wait in the tryst of the cool amethyst for the recreant maiden of day !
But hark ! 't is a horn !
But list to the chant of the dawn !
There is thrill, there is whisper of morn !
The unseen Conqueror whirls his skirmish of lancers afar on the lawn !

Hark, from afar to the jubilee reverberating !
Hist ! 'T is the tune of the dancers of the sky !
Mark where yon star like a pillared flame is coruscating !
List while the croon of the eons flutters by !
Pause as ye kneel,
Feel
For the fingers of a sympathetic past that lingers !
Kneel, and beseech,
Reach
For the tresses of a future's virginal caresses !
Reach
Till the passion of your speech
Dies away on far horizons like a tide upon a beach !
Kneel
With a sacrament's appeal

   While the will of the Supreme
Lifts the planet-folded curtain from the secret of His
   dream ;
Wakes the consecrated ages with the breaking of His seal !

  " O morning of glory ! O wonderful story !
   We shall see the gold roofs where the sunlight is
    gleaming ! " —
List ! 'T is the doom of an ominous delay ! —
  " Nay, flames of the land in their joy transitory
   Shall melt in realities sweeter than dreaming." —
Hark ! 'T is the gloom of a wing upon the gray ! —
  " Vast temples like palms shall o'ertop the blue moun-
   tains.
   Fair maidens shall kneel on the beeches like wil-
    lows." —
Hist ! 'T is the spume of the sirens in the bay ! —
  " And sages like gods shall recline where cool fountains
   Fling down their gold braids to the breasts of the
    billows." —
Mark ! 't is the plume of the demon of the spray ! —

   " O tense expectation ! "
Now, heave once again with thy travail, vast womb of the
   Earth !
   " O dawn of salvation ! "
Thine offspring, the Sun, hath awakened. He burns to
   the birth !

"O dance through my blood!"
The legions of vapors have snatched him, and wrapped
    him in fire!
"Shout flames to the flood!"
He reigns like a God on the throne of their hottest
    desire!

    Parched by his sovereign blast
    The siren of the sea-mist breaks
Her tangled coils in lingering golden flakes
That swirl in dimming breath athwart the pennon on the
    mast.
The stranger Tritons lean in gaping crowds,
Hanging on bowsprits, flocking like nesting gulls among
    the shrouds,
    Peering in breathless wonder through
For emerald sheens to streak the mottled marquetry
    of blue.
      "Dost see it?" "No,
'T was but the lazy turtle of a cloud-bank low
    Pawing the murky tide." —
"There! in yon purple whale that looms his verge
    Upon the starboard side!"
"Can you not hear the muffled gulping of the surge,
  As if some slimy passion monster-lipped
Over the naked bosom of a sandbar slipped?" —
  "Hush! for the yeoman sun now ploughs
    His yoked quadruple team
Where wingèd flocks upon the steaming upland
    browse!" —

"O jewelled gleam
Of diamond lace that droops upon a throbbing rosy
    neck!"
"Look where the braided fleck
Of foaming breath in spangles
Leaps like a toying hand that tangles
The fringe of palmy hair upon the reefs!"
"Now,— now
The curtain lifts,— and lifts!"
"We shall behold, perchance, the beetling brow
Of snowland drifts!"
"O thrills!" "O joys!" — "O griefs!
'T is but a desert wilderness of level staring greens!"
"There are no crystal sheens,
Or azure-skirted clouds of inland peaks!
Only a few familiar creeks
That loll with listless arm against the drowsy bosom of
    the land!" —
"Yet is it God's own strand!
Crescents of solid blessing bounding this slippery salt
    abyss!
O, I could fling a million-wingéd kiss
To every lisping leaf that croons in the lap of yon
    palms!
Ye crested doves of calms!" —
"Away! below! away!
Don proudest daintiest array
To grace this first glad Christian holiday,
This first mad feast
Drunk with the plighted East!"

"Quick float
The passion-breasted curve of each eager boat!"
"Stand, and be wrapped in
The imperial flag of thy monarchs, Captain!
Sailors, salute again
This first vice-regal reign!
Behold your Cosmos-conqueror, the vested Admiral of
Spain!"

O blessed astronomer!
Who, fired with hope,
Point'st the spear-gathering eye of thy telescope
To some miscalculated altitude of dark;
Where yet thine eye shall mark
An unexpected new-waked planet stir
Upon a stranger arc;—
Now, thou, O Neptune's priest!
Whose blood-drawn charts like polished lenses magnify
Thine altars of the East;
Though thy swift prow may fly
Straight through the vast impossible as an arrow-beam of
light,
Yet hast thou struck a dark unreckoned orb that bars thy
flight.
The very failure of thy bitter shame
Shall lend a starry splendor to thy name!

Now, streaking through the tide
As avalanches slide

Down the blue-green enamel of the hills,
    Each petrel shallop thrills
To blooded brawn that sledges at the tholes ;
    And lips of parching souls
Suck the warm greens of fancy's tender juices.
    Up through the palm-fringed sluices
Where amorous Atlantic pouts his melting mouth
  Steeped in the spicy ardors of the South
    Against twin coral lips,
  Where the warm-blooded island sips
The trembling passion of his lazy swoons
Through the hot fanning of the naked noons,
    The helmsmen steer.
The liquid languor of the atmosphere
Adopts them, laps them to the milky softness of its bosom.
    They see white cups of lilies blossom
Their brimming hearts away in odor of a lotus dream.
    Where now a clear cool stream
Sifts through its crystal hair the golden minnows of the sand,
    They beach upon the land.

    Gliding through the palm leaves,
      Crouching 'neath the grasses,
    Where the liquid calm leaves
      Shadow as it passes,
        Flash of raven tresses !
        Chestnut nakednesses !
      Vain the guesses,
    Be they forest lads or lasses.

No Paynims, these ;
Or polished ivory Chinese ;
Nor Ethiopian imps
Scanned through the snake-like glimpse
Of Afric's murky river !
Crested with butterfly plume, and a rainbow-wingéd
quiver,
And smeared with melting drops of golden rings, —
a prize
For salt-encrusted eyes, —
A leopard-lithe and cypress-stalwart chief
Breaks from his covert tawninesses of banana leaf;
And, with the timid bronzes of his train,
Prostrates himself before these white immortals of the
main. —
Two cherished streams from primal human fount,
Parted by some far prehistoric mount,
To flow in one another on forever
One double-tinted river
From this first moment of fraternal years ! —
Now doth the Admiral, prince among his peers,
Flash to the cloudland shore amid the crimsons of Olym-
pian splendor ;
As when the sun alights with glances tender
Upon the purple passion-world of skied Acropolis.
And from the radiate prows they leap, as canopies
Of jewelled clouds to tent their monarch's glory. —
Up from the glooms of Aryan shadows hoary
They flock like gilded cormorants, and swoop

Upon the eel-like shore. A steel-winged troop
Of God's avengers, sword in hand, they swirl.
Above their viking heads embroidered battle-flags
    unfurl.
And hymns swell fan-like from the templed sod
To bless the Mother of these gods' own God.
Then doth Columbus kneel, and lave his face
In the warm billowy bosom of the bridal sands.
And stately are the loyal words that grace
Their twin-locked monarchs' memory. He stands
One instant, like a king that grasps all space : —
Then walks in silence down the savage shore.
And time flows on as placid as before.

Ah, hero ! hast thou felt
A shadow of the darkness like a belt
Folding thee close? And wilt thou press it down
Upon thy forehead, like a thorny crown?
And dost thou sense the martyred blood-drops
    trickle,
Thou fruiting ripeness for the Reaper's sickle?

* * * * * *

O what is it lurks in the heart of the diamond atoms of
    time, like a pestilent poison brewing?
Hark ! 'T is the undertone of demons as they mock !
What querulous scud of an ominous storm through the
    creaking portals of purpose is whining and mewing?

Hist! 'T is the wings of the elemental flock!
List! 'T is the whetting of their swords upon the rock!
O blast of disruption, O jealousy pale, now the skeleton
   lair of thine ultimate evil unlock!

O shriek of defiance, of hate that endangers thin bonds
   of the continents double;
Defiant despair with its gathering charges of blackness, as
   hurricanes bubble
From founts of the glacial granite, and grimly annihilate
   time with their trouble!
Now hark to the hiss of this garrulous crew the swift doom
   of their madness pursuing! —
"Yes, press us, ye tyrants of gods, if ye dare! We 've
   enough of your secret undoing.
Have you thrown us as hostage these wretches of Span-
   iards to torture and crush in our maw,
As once long ago you were forced to surrender your
   crucified King of the Law?
This world is our own; and no hint of its wealth shall go
   back with your robbers to Spain.
We Titans, and dragons, and gorgons, and vultures, and
   slimy green crabs of the main,
We send you a bat for our herald to parley! Quick, yield
   to our right, or be slain!"

O crests of the morning! O blades of the gloaming!
   O knights of the splendor! O Lords of Creation!

The nebulous squadrons of chargers are foaming;
    And legions wheel out from each far constellation.
The blood of the martyred lends spur to their valor.
    No Paladins strong as the Christs who have died!
O tremble, ye myrmidon braggarts of pallor,
    And kiss the steel glove of the God ye defied!

Now, hurled like a hurricane hand when it reaches wild
    grasp for the zenith of noons,
Then combing like tides thunders down on the world with
    the snarl of embattled typhoons,
Mid crests of sea-horses that spume to Cimmerian skies
    their hoar ices of sprays,
Or, sucked to the depths of maelstroms, gulp down the
    rich boil of Tellurian blaze; —
So swung the sheen-crescents of Michael that swept with
    bent tails to the uttermost stars;
So legions of lightning split opulent space with their crests
    of beatified Mars;
And flung the dread weight of Olympian wills on the chat-
    tering hordes of the devils! —
O fierce coruscations of ranks superposed, gold on gold,
    flaming levels on levels
Over stratified crests of the steeled chevaliers their auroras
    of spectral dishevels! —
As they mount where the hoofs of victorious steeds thunder
    sparks from the flint of their helms,
As they mount, as they mount like the scaling of tides to
    the rims of Cyclopean realms,

Where the fumes of their manes sweep away with the
    silver of scud to the swash of the skies ; —
Now damn with the vengeance of dominant doom, and
    the quench of the blood in your cries
Those green crumpled lights of a serpentine gloom in the
    hollows of impotent eyes ; —
Till, chained in some vast subterranean tomb where En-
    celadus scoffs at their sighs,
He shall stifle with curds of crude matter their insolent
    wrangle and chatter ;
Where the dragons that trail with the imps shall be shrunk
    to the crawling of shrimps,
And inordinate blasts of typhoons lie encaged like limp
    gas in balloons !
For the faith of the True in the New is as sure as the God
    in the blue ;
And the seeds of corruption breed cold in the gangrenous
    limbs of the old.
And though heroes be butchered by scores, and their
    bodies be sown to the mould,
Yet the blood of the Christs silvers up in the lilies of
    Easter, and gold
Streaks the eve of Gethsemane's sweat with the splendors
    of purpose untold !

        O hark,
           From afar !
        'T is a lark !
           'T is a star !

'T is the star of salvation that rides like a king through the
triumphal arches of noon with the sun in his car!

    But list
      To the tune
    Of the mist
    In a swoon,
As it hooks its bent horns with the stratified islands of
palms like the floating white wraith of a mariner-
moon!

    But kneel
      Where they reach
    Like a keel
    On a beach,
As they plant a strange foot at the root of a cactus that
weeps bloody blossoms too heavenly fragrant for
speech!

    O sing
      With the hymn!
    As a wing
    Let it swim
In a curving blue wake through the dissonant billows of
space to the Virgin enthroned with her pink cher-
ubim!

    O hark! O hark! O pray,
Ye dear warm lingering faiths of a dying day!

O day unparalleled on couch of rosy feathers dying,
    Thy elemental voices still are prophesying.
    Still shall the tuneful sirens of the deep
    Drag thy triumphal car that rides sublime
        Over the irridescent waves of Time
To where new curtained continents fore'er recede, and sleep.
        O hark!   O hark!
Over the globing oceans slide thy last immensities of arc.—
    Now hath thy true astronomer and priest
    Reached o'er the darkling bar with free-built arch
    Where we shall see his grander purpose march
Round flaming inward altars to the crystal-hearted East.
    His triumph is not bounded
By the vast bustle of this world of stepping-stones he founded;
    But by the consummation of his plan
        To weave all creeds
    And teeming blossoms of the rarest human seeds
To deck the tomb-throned Union of his Monarchy of Man!

        But buzzing croons
    That whizz among the gurgles of bassoons,
        Where curly pearls
        In vortices of whorls
  Scoff like demonic faces in the moons;
        Or sibilant shimmers

That hang low branches of their palmy glimmers
To mummer mimics of the lullabied lagoons;—
These still
Up-spill
From sulphurous chasms
The spurting spasms
Of incorrigible will;
Like buzzing flies
That choose where noonday dries
The slimy ooze of greening marshes for their minstrelsies;
Or crocodiles that snooze with snorting cries,
Or hissing drag
Their scaly lengths a-swish among the shivers of sweet flag.

And is there then no end of stifled woe?
We do not know.
We can but keep the faith
Even when sucked between the shredded jaws of death;—
Even as he,
The first and last begotten hero of the sea.
We can but let the twofold music sigh, and die away;
As if a maiden's hand
Led some dark shipwrecked thing along the strand
Until their voices blended with the evanescent murmur
of the spray.
So now all subtlest natures seem
To melt upon the soft etherial bliss of the Supreme.
And perfect silence turns the numbered pages of a dying
theme.

NOTES.

"O sweet dead artist and seer." — p. 14.

Kano Hogai, into whose mouth I put the following summary of Eastern life, was the greatest Japanese painter of recent times, a genius whose penetration to the heart of early oriental ideals seemed like special inspiration. He was for years one of my dearest friends, and in Japanese art my most valued teacher. I have represented him as the re-incarnate spirit of oriental art. His death in 1888 was a national calamity.

"Where the orange temples of Kásŭga shine." — p. 14.

The ancient city of Nara, the capital of Japan in the eighth century, still glories in a grove of mighty pines and cedars which sweep away for a mile to the Eastern mountains, sheltering the dainty buildings of the great Shinto temple, Kásŭga. Wild streams have torn narrow beds through it. Venerable Buddhist monasteries flank it on the north. Archæologically, Nara is the treasure-house of Japan. There in the spring and summer of 1886 I spent with Hogai many weeks in delightful study.

"Which the snow-clad virgins in cloister dim." — p. 15.

These maidens of Kásŭga are consecrated to the service of the gods, and at intervals celebrate the symbolic dance called "Kagura."

"Mid statues of Buddha the meek." — p. 16.

Hogai first visits the North Indian capital of the Scythian king, Kanishka, who about the beginning of the Christian era held the first Council of Northern Buddhism, whence the canon was later disseminated to Central and Eastern Asia. At this Cashmerian centre, in an outburst of creative fervor, the new ideals of a rich and profound faith, large enough in its plan to satisfy the spiritual needs of a continent, were first adequately externalized in forms of Hellenic derivation. Many fine relics of this so-called Greco-Buddhist sculpture, including a haughty portrait statue of the Tartar Constantine himself, have been excavated, and are mostly preserved in the museum at Lahore.

"The great Vasubandhu to mark." — p. 16.

Vasubandhu, the greatest follower of Nagarjuna, and one of the most important patriarchs in the line of esoteric transmission, was a man whose extraordinary spiritual and intellectual endowments enabled him largely to mould the subsequent course of Northern Buddhism, much as St. Paul did that of Christianity. He is the author of numerous works which remain to-day a corner-stone of Japanese Buddhism. It is not certain whether in old age he was present at the Northern Synod; but his spirit was doubtless dominant in the person of its president, his disciple Vasumitra. A portrait statue of Vasubandhu, preserved in Nara, shows us a face of enormous power.

"Now moss like a pall." — p. 16.

When the Chinese pilgrim Hiouentsang visited these sacred seats in the seventh century, he found them already in pitiful ruin. The Greco-Buddhist relics which he brought to China became the germ of a lofty religious art throughout the Tang Dynasty, and in Corea and Japan during the eighth century. A trace of this Hellenic quality has never died out in the art of the latter country.

"Back to thy pious imperial prince." — p. 17.

Hogai refers to Taitsong the Great, the second Emperor of Tang, through whose toleration Buddhism was to make rapid strides; and, speaking of himself as one of Kanishka's sculptors, he predicts his rebirth as Godoshi (Wutaotse), the greatest religious painter of Tang.

"Gather these Bodhisats,
And battle-scarred features of grim Arhats." — p. 17.

These are the titles of two degrees in Buddhist saintship. The Arhat, in Northern Buddhism, is one who has attained only subjective purification by withdrawing from the world. He bears marks of the severity of his ascetic discipline. A Bodhisattwa is one who, through the passion of divine love for men, has mingled with the evil of the world and overcome it, thus winning a leadership in the overshadowing army of the good. He is represented as of beautiful face and heavenly mien.

"And the masterful heads of Scythian knights." — p. 17.

These are the four archangels militant, whose statues stand at the corner of every ancient altar. They are represented as stamping on evil in the form of a distorted imp. There can be little doubt that the military costume of these figures in early Chinese and Japanese examples is borrowed from the trappings of ancient Scythian generals. The finest specimens extant are at Kaidanin of Nara, modelled in clay, of life size, and dating from the commencement of the eighth century.

"Blue gods unmoved in everlasting flame." — p. 18.

The art of the Tang Dynasty became strongest in religious painting. Symbolic figures of large size and mystic import were painted on the walls of temples in firm outline and rich color. Of these the Bodhisattwa Fudo, whose name signifies "The Unmoved," was depicted as blue, and seated in the midst of orange flame. The colors, halos, flames, and clouds of such paintings, represent the spiritual aura, currents, and conditions generated by these lofty beings.

"Black bronze in an infinite mould." — p. 18.

The highest creative power of Northern Buddhistic art was reached in early Japanese bronze sculpture, which clothes with the dignity and beauty of a Greek reminiscence the noblest suggestions of superhuman spiritual types. The finest remains are the colossal statues in the temple Yakushiji, near Nara, cast in the eighth century, of a metal which in color resembles polished ebony.

"O crystalline flash at the bar of billows." — p. 18.

Hogai now transfers the scene of his description to China. I have chosen from the several periods of Chinese culture that most typically artistic one of the later Sung Dynasty, whose idealistic outburst of Buddhist illumination in the twelfth century rendered its capital, Hangchow, a birthplace of inspired forms. Marco Polo describes the city as he saw it some years later, and we have minute contemporary records of it in Chinese poetry and painting. It lay a few miles inland, between the Sientang Estuary and the beautiful "Western Lake," surrounded by groves and picturesque mountains, among whose nooks and crags grew mossy temples and secluded villas, where worked the artists, poets, statesmen, and philosophers of that golden age. The flavor of its intense life I have attempted to suggest in the following passage.

"Of soul in the infinite warmth of things." — p. 19.

The central mood of this Chinese idealism, drawn from the Zen (Dhyan), or contemplative sect of Buddhists, was the vital realization of nature as a storehouse of spiritual forms. Not by way of cold abstraction, or of a labored symbolism, but as seen in flashes of devout insight, did the world become to man a mirror of his own soul. Never elsewhere has the passion of faith inspired such a profound study of external beauties. It is the well of oriental landscape-art.

"There Love is a law, and the Law is an art." — p. 20.

Here too the noble Eastern theory of the "musical" relation of human beings to one another in a heaven-ordained spiritual brotherhood received for a time its most notable realization.

"Farewell to the dawn in the meadow." — p. 21.

Hogai now expressly transfers the picture to his native Japan in a lament for its vanishing glory and innocence. I have tried in the following pages to realize something of the delicate charm and significance of Japanese life and art at their best. Here is a flavor so subtle as to elude direct expression. It was the perfect striking of an extreme note in the scale of human culture.

"Leap of the carp." — p. 26.

Well-known scenes of Japanese out-door life are referred to on this page. At the garden of Kameido, near Tokio, a wonderful trellis of low-hanging wistaria is thrown across a temple pool stocked with fish. The shrine is dedicated to the scholar Michizane, in whose worship the faithful cow has become a symbol.

"Basking like kittens in the love of their mothers." — p. 25.

One who has been admitted to the intimacy of Japanese households, regrets the untrustworthiness of some authorities who declare this people devoid of family life and affection.

"Pray to the holy snow-white Queen." — p. 25.

This is the Bodhisattwa Kuannon, the beautiful female spirit of Providential Love, as represented in contemplation on a rock by the sea.

"The Buddha of Infinite Light." — p. 26.

I refer to Amida. As the central blinding Splendor of the universe, he approximates to the Christian conception of God the Creator.

"One priest white-robed who seemed to glide." — p. 27.

His Reverence the Archbishop Keitoku, of the Tendai sect at Miidera temple on Lake Biwa, I still look up to as my most inspired and devoutly liberal teacher in matters religious. Precious were the days and nights I had the privilege of spending with him in the vicinities of Kioto, Nara, and Nikko. He was a lofty living exemplar of the spiritual knighthood. He passed from the visible form in 1889.

"Since the days when Kukai hurled
His dart from the Chinese world." — p. 27.

Kukai, or Kobo Daishi, one of the three great founders of Esoteric Buddhism in Japan, spent many years of his youth in study at a famous Chinese monastery. About to return to his native country early in the ninth century, he meditated long concerning the site of his projected temple. Leaving the decision to the powers of heaven, he is said to have thrown his *vagra*, or metal mace, into the air in the direction of Japan, whither it was borne by divine means, and lodged in a tall tree on the top of Koya mountain. Here after his return it was found by the Daishi, and here he built the splendid monastery of Koyasan, which remains to this day the patriarchal seat of the Shingon sect in Japan.

"This for the *world*, as for Japan." — p. 28.

The Archbishop Keitoku believed that the Western spirit was nearly ripe to receive the lofty doctrine which Eastern guardians have preserved for its precious legacy.

"Expansive self-willed personality." — p. 29.

It will be perceived that I oppose personality, the self-centred and self-originated will of an incarnate man, to individuality, the unconscious strength and freedom of an intelligence immersed in the divinity of its work. One is peculiar through the abstract isolation of subjectivity ; the other is peculiar through the infinite fulness of the well of Spirit whence it flows.

"O self-fed spring of thought." — p. 33.

The following passage personifies the round of the sciences in terms of their characteristic work. Evolved in self-expansion, they yet build compensating structures of world-wide toleration.

"Before the judges of Manwantaras." — p. 34.

A Manwantara is the immense total period of bloom in a manifested universe.

"Holding the poisoned cup to Mongol lips." — p. 35.

I refer to the opium trade with China. After all, it is the selfish expansiveness of commerce, rather than warfare or science, which discharges the decreed function of bearing the West back into the bosom of the East. It is the last service of the explosive life of competition.

"See in last glimpse how unchecked years condense
 The forces of destruction." — p. 35.

I conceived the tragic incident of the storming of the Summer Palace at Peking to typify the central irony of the situation — the knights of the West in blind ignorance smiting the very princess of the East whom they were destined to espouse.

"O spirit of Genghis Khan." — p. 40.

It should be noted that the excesses of Western custom introduced into Tokio society previous to the year 1888 are now rapidly on the wane. The picture of contradictions which I witnessed is not overdrawn. We may be thankful that the era of confusion is already melting away into that of reconstruction.

"And here come art students with honors." — p. 41.

For years in a government university, Japanese artists were taught the technique of Western painting, sculpture, and architecture by European professors. For the time, native "barbarian" arts were despised and neglected. The absurdities of the hybrid system of teaching drawing in Japanese public schools cannot be exaggerated. But these are now things of the past.

"And Roshi who looks at the cracks
 On terrapins' backs." — p. 41.

Roshi (the Japanese pronunciation of Laotse) was the Plato of China, whose idealistic system later Taoist followers have reduced to a species of divination and magic.

"Why, they blush as they think of the foxes." — p. 41.

Foxes in Japan were believed to be at times the incarnation of mischievous elemental spirits.

> "Let thy heel with diamond lightning
> Blast the eyelids of the Beast." — p. 52.

Here I refer to the forms of the archangels mentioned in a previous note. The *vagra*, or mace, also spoken of, has its Chinese name sometimes translated by the word "diamond." Here the diamond, in its hardness and concentration of ray, may symbolically express the spiritual potency of the instrument.

"THE WOOD DOVE." — p. 81.

The refrain of this poem attempts to render the peculiar pathetic rhythm of the oriental wood dove's note, which breaks off at last in the midst of a measure.